INTRODUCTION TO TYPOGRAPHY

OLIVER SIMON

INTRODUCTION TO TYPOGRAPHY

edited by

DAVID BLAND

> The old artists of the classical school were never egotists. Egotism has been and remains responsible for many defects of modern typography. *Talbot Baines Reed*

LONDON
FABER AND FABER

First published in mcmxlv by
Faber & Faber Limited
24 Russell Square, London, W.C.1
Revised and Published in this
new edition mcmlxiii
Printed in Great Britain
at The Curwen Press, Plaistow

EDITOR'S NOTE

The author of this book was a purist and it is this quality that gives his instructions their peculiar bite and authority. But it caused him also to ignore certain technical developments in printing of which he instinctively seems to have disapproved, for instance the increasing use of slug-setting and film-setting for bookwork.

To make the book of more contemporary use it seemed essential to mention these things at least, and to show examples of them so that the student can judge them for himself. In addition, several new title-pages and jackets (some designed by the author himself) have been added.

Of my own alterations and additions I have only included those in the text (and they are by far the more numerous) which agree with Oliver Simon's own tenets. Where I disagree or wish to indicate that there are other opinions I have put them in a signed footnote.

D.B.

ACKNOWLEDGEMENTS

In addition to the acknowledgements made in previous editions, the editor would like to thank the following:

Mr. Herbert Simon and The Curwen Press for co-operation in the preparation and printing of this book.

The Monotype Corporation and the Linotype and Intertype Companies for type specimens on pages 14–24 and 121–2. Stephenson Blake for specimens on pages 56, 121 and 122. The Westerham Press for decorations on page 135.

The Limited Editions Club, the Nonesuch Press, the Oxford and Cambridge University Presses, Faber & Faber, Hamish Hamilton, Chatto and Windus, Lund Humphries and Penguin Books for permission to reproduce title-pages on pages 74–88.

Oxford University Press, The Cresset Press, Penguin, Methuen and Faber & Faber for binding and cover designs on pages 115 and 117.

Hamish Hamilton, Weidenfeld & Nicholson, Faber & Faber, the Oxford University Press and Eyre & Spottiswoode for jackets on pages 124–9.

Book Design and Production for the loan of a block on page 117, and The Bodley Head for permission to reproduce a page on page 110.

CONTENTS

DEFINITIONS OF TYPOGRAPHY

SEVENTEENTH CENTURY

'By a Typographer, I do not mean a Printer, as he is Vulgarly accounted, any more than Dr. Dee means a Carpenter or Mason to be an Architect: but by a Typographer, I mean such a one, who by his own Judgement, from solid reasoning with himself, can either perform, or direct others to perform from the beginning to the end, all the Handy-works and Physical Operations relating to Typographie.'

Mechanick Exercises, or the Doctrine of Handy-works applied to the Art of Printing
By Joseph Moxon. 1683

EIGHTEENTH CENTURY

'Typography may be regarded as consisting of three parts, each distinct and indispensable, namely, punch-cutting, founding and printing. The practice of the different branches produces artists of three different kinds, the first punch-cutters, the second founders and the third printers, but he who combines a knowledge of all three branches is fit to be styled a *Typographer*.'

Manuel Typographique
By Simon-Pierre Fournier. 1764 (Translation)

NINETEENTH CENTURY

'Typography: Typographical execution; the arrangement of composed type, or the appearance of printed matter.'

The Standard Dictionary. 1890

TWENTIETH CENTURY

'Typography may be defined as the craft of rightly disposing printing material in accordance with specific purpose; of so arranging the letters, distributing the space and controlling the type as to aid to the maximum the reader's comprehension of the text. . . . Typography is the efficient means to an essentially utilitarian and only accidentally æsthetic end, for the enjoyment of patterns is rarely the reader's chief aim. Therefore, any disposition of printing material which, whatever the intention, has the effect of coming between author and reader is wrong.'

First Principles of Typography
By Stanley Morison. 1935

INTRODUCTION

PRINTING is a way of life. It can transcend the boundaries of a trade and can take its place as one of the arts when the presiding genius at the printing office combines within himself the roles of business man, scholar, and artist. If he lacks business acumen and knowledge of the mechanics of the craft, the printing office must inevitably languish and finally cease to function. If he has not acquired a sufficient degree of scholarship, he cannot successfully attempt to be a book printer in the fullest sense of the term. If he is not something of an artist, he cannot hope to evolve and maintain a typographic style. These three qualities are seldom combined in one person, but the printer who is endowed with them is eligible for his place in the history of printing.

The study of the history of printing is important, for it is the masterpieces of the past that point a way to the contribution we, of this generation, can make to typographic art and practice. The fame and achievements of Aldus, Simon de Colines, the Estiennes, Jean de Tournes, Vascosan, Plantin, Baskerville, Bodoni, the early Didots, Bulmer and Bensley, and many others, remain with us as an inspiration and a stimulus. Their best works are not only an unfailing source of pleasure but, in their typographic style, an expression of the civilization to which they were themselves an indispensable contribution.

Book typography has enriched the European scene for some five hundred years and continues to do so in our own time. Millions of books have been printed since the invention of printing. Many of these, admittedly, have been the humdrum efforts of ordinary tradesmen bent on making a living, but some books have been conceived with something more than the mere minimum of competence needed for strictly utilitarian and trade purposes. They have disclosed themselves to us and won our hearts through the excellence of their typographic style. This minority has been with us since the invention of printing, and will always be with us in greater or lesser degree.

ix

Over fifteen thousand books of various kinds are printed in this country every year; they comprise Bibles, Art Books, Fiction, Children's Books, Biographies, Autobiographies, Poetry, Plays, Histories, Scientific and Technical Books, Political Books, Text-books and School Books, and many more, including the vast circulation of reprints of the Classics. A casual visitor to a book-shop would observe that all the books to be seen followed, superficially at least, a more or less definite convention in sizes and typography, and that the printing was either good, bad, or indifferent. In our present period, for instance, it would be noted that all novels are large or small crown 8vo, most biographies and autobiographies demy 8vo, which are sizes governed by the demands of public libraries. There would, for the same reason, be a certain similarity in thickness and, although the lettering on binding cases might vary in style, nearly all these books would be bound in boards and (apart from paperbacks) only a small number in wrappers. Again, an overwhelming majority of the books set on the Monotype machine would appear to our observer to have a further element in common since only the current Monotype book faces available to the printer would be seen.

These rough-and-ready conventions of each period are necessary both for the practical management of the printing, publishing and bookselling trades and, not least, for the establishment of a high degree of easy legibility for the reader. The need of achieving such easy legibility is one of the main reasons why typographic changes are slow in coming about.

One striking change of our own time has been the mechanization of type-setting. Nevertheless it has taken more than a generation[1] for hand-setting to be completely abandoned in favour of mechanical setting. The Monotype Corporation and the Linotype and Inter-type Companies, who make the machines and matrices for mechan-ical type-setting for printers in this country, have, by gradual stages, introduced fresh type faces suitable to their machines and agreeable

[1] The Monotype machine became available in 1896.

to the readers of books. Slug-setting by Linotype or Intertype is almost exclusively used in America for bookwork but in Britain the Monotype machine is more widely employed. Film-setting by Monophoto, Lumitype, etc. is rapidly approaching perfection and will eventually have a powerful effect on typography as well as on the printer's finances. It produces its type image photographically by enlarging or reducing from a prototype. This tends to blur the finer points of type design as described in this book (see page 29).

Paper also is now almost entirely machine-made, with the consequent disappearance of the 'deckle edge', a change that makes for convenience as well as cleanliness. The 'finish' of machine-made paper is relatively smooth, so that the practice of damping paper preparatory to printing has ceased to be necessary. Excellent presswork can be achieved on good machine-made papers, an excellence no less desirable although different from that achieved by presswork on damped hand-made paper.

Binding cases have become simple in design, largely through the rapid mechanization of the binding trade which has so far, unlike printing, outstripped the binding trade's capacity to take much initiative in design. The book-jacket has become a necessity and offers a rich field for decoration. It keeps the books themselves clean in transit from printer to reader and, appropriately designed, has proved to be a first-class salesman and a valuable means of propaganda both for the publisher and the author. There are many other changes; we have merely touched on a few in an attempt to indicate how change comes about partly from the *outside*—the printer following the needs of the reader as new habits and conditions appear.

The printer and publisher can initiate change from the *inside*, for the typographic medium is, by its very nature and through the large choice of type faces and materials, subtly flexible. The full practice of Typography is an unending process of learning and a challenge to individual skill, imagination and common sense, but this need not imply exhibitionism; authentic printing has no need to proclaim itself. Authors, too, have been known for their influence on Typography,[1] while the demands of a mass of typographically conscious readers do not fail to exert a certain pressure.

There are many excellent books on Type Design, as well as the History, the Mechanics and the Technics of Printing, and we shall not bring coals to Newcastle by covering the ground again, except incidentally. It is our endeavour rather to describe as briefly as possible from our own experience some of the many typographic fundamentals of book-production.

[1] See *The Printing of Books*, 'The Author and his Printer', by Holbrook Jackson. 1938.

INTRODUCTION TO TYPOGRAPHY

I

FOUNDATIONS

EXAMINATION of a well-produced book will show that a successful combination of its main essentials of type face, composition,
margins, paper, presswork and binding forms an harmonious and
legible whole. To achieve harmony and legibility is the main
object of typography. This needs knowledge, skill and discipline
—knowledge of type and traditions of printing—skill to assemble
and manipulate the raw materials of book production—discipline
to choose imaginatively what is appropriate and consistent.

For the practice of typography we must have men and tools—
in other words, a well-trained staff and a well-equipped printing
office. It is more difficult to obtain the former than the latter.
That is an old problem, and we are reminded of an advertisement
inserted by John Bell in the issue of *The World*, of 11 July 1787,
which reads:

PRESSMEN FOR BOOK-WORK

Wanted, Four Complete Press-men, who can execute Book-work in the
most perfect manner, and who can be warranted for their regularity and
sobriety. They may depend on constant employment so long as they
execute their business perfectly; they will be paid by the piece or by the
week, as may be most conducive to their own interest, and the satisfaction
of their employer.

Composition, Presswork and Proof-reading should indeed be
of the highest standard possible, nor is it sufficient to have only
a knowledge of printing practice and history; we must go
further and make ourselves acquainted with the conditions of
business of those we work for, namely the publisher and bookseller, who in their turn must not neglect the habits and just
requirements of the reader.

I

Each printing office will have its own House Rules, and these rules will no doubt vary in detail between one House and another. Indeed, this is as it should be; books are written in many varieties, and there are in consequence various solutions to some of the typographical problems that arise. We have in this book occasionally submitted our own predilections for practices that are by no means uniform throughout the printing trade, notably in the matter of quotation marks, in the use of which our two oldest University Presses are divided. It is not infrequent for a publisher to have his own House Rules too, which the printer may in some cases be obliged to follow, even if they contradict some points in his own. A printer's House Rules are, however, effective on most occasions; indeed, if they are wisely drafted they are more often than not accepted with gratitude. Furthermore, there is no doubt that they make for cohesion amongst the staff both old and new, which in turn produces the rudiments of a recognizable printing style. With these few general observations in mind, we can first of all present in this book some simple rules of composition for printers. We shall then examine step by step some of the many problems likely to present themselves to the printer on receipt of an average manuscript.

RULES OF COMPOSITION

SPELLING AND PUNCTUATION

THE carefully prepared MS. of a precise author must be strictly followed as to punctuation and spelling, so also must extracts quoted from other works. Many writers leave some of the details of punctuation of their copy to the printer. An intelligent interpretation of an author's meaning by means of correctly placed punctuation marks is an art that can be acquired only by long experience, and for which no hard-and-fast rules can be formulated. Many valuable hints on spelling, punctuation, italicizing, capitalization, divisions of words, and other matters of style, are to be found in the Oxford Rules[1] which can be taken mostly as a standard authority. Collins's Dictionary[2] gives useful hints on the italicizing of foreign words, abbreviations, and unusual spellings, and contains much useful biographical and geographical information. Titles, displayed lines, chapter heads, running head-lines, page heads, dates, captions to blocks, the names of speakers in plays (where these occupy a line to themselves), are not to be followed by a full point.

QUOTATION MARKS

Use single quotation marks (') outside and double (") only for quotations within quotations. If there should be another quotation within the second, use the single quotation marks. Where long extracts are indented or set in smaller type, quotation marks are not to be used. Punctuation marks used at the end of a quoted passage must be inside the quotation marks if they belong to the

[1] *Rules for Compositors and Readers at the University Press, Oxford.* 36th Edition. 1957.
[2] *Authors' and Printers' Dictionary,* by F. Howard Collins. 10th Edition. 1960.

quotation, otherwise outside. When isolated words or an incomplete sentence are quoted the punctuation mark is placed outside the 'quotes', with the exception of the interrogation mark (?) and the exclamation (!), which are placed inside the 'quotes' if they belong to the quotation. When a quotation is complete, the 'quotes' are placed outside the full point.

PARENTHESES AND BRACKETS

Parentheses ( ) are used chiefly to denote interpolations, and brackets [ ] are used to show notes or explanations, or words assumed to be omitted from original MSS. and added by subsequent editors. They may also be used to indicate the correct spelling of a mis-spelt word.

Occasionally parentheses are needed within parentheses and although it is sometimes recommended to use them thus (( )), it is our opinion that the subsidiary interpolation is more clearly shown by the use of brackets within the parentheses thus ([ ]). Where the bracket and parenthesis fall together at the end, a thin space should be inserted between them.

CAPITALIZATION

No definite rules can be laid down for the use of initial capitals. When rightly used they give emphasis to important words to which the author wishes to give prominence, and the carefully prepared MS. of the writer who knows what he wants must be strictly followed. Here are a few of the more familiar words in common use where the initial capital is usual:

His Majesty, Dark Ages, London Clay, Bagshot Beds, Upper Greensand (in geology), Lady Day, Berkeley Square.

Denominational terms and names of parties, as Baptist, Presbyterian, Liberal, Conservative, Socialist, Fascist.

Nature, Time, Death, and other abstract nouns when personified, e.g.: O Death, where is thy sting?

When a person is addressed by his rank instead of by name, an initial capital letter is used, e.g.: 'Good morning, Colonel.'

'Oh, Father, how delightful it is to be home again! How is Mother, and where is she?' *but* 'Your mother (l.c.) is in the garden, little dreaming of the surprise awaiting her.'

Capitalize pronouns and synonyms referring to the Deity: Almighty, Christ, Father, God, He, Himself, His, Jehovah, Lord, Me, Mine, Thee, the Holy Trinity, Thine, Thy; *but* who, whom, whose (l.c.).

Figure, Number, Plate (Fig., No., Pl.) should each begin with a capital letter.

Do not use capital S or E, etc., in such expressions as southern Italy, eastern Europe. But names of *political divisions* such as Southern Rhodesia, Northern Ireland, Western Australia, should have initial capitals.

SMALL CAPITALS

Small capitals are used for the purpose of giving more emphasis to a word or sentence than can be conveyed by printing the same in italic. They may also be employed for chapter headings and head-lines, and for various purposes of display in the preliminaries of a book. Small capitals should be letter-spaced.

ITALIC

Italic is used for emphasis and for the names of books, magazines, newspapers, films, plays, and operas, appearing in the text; also for foreign words and phrases; but extracts from foreign texts, however short, should be in roman. The title of an article from a magazine should be in roman, 'quoted', and the name of the magazine itself in italic. Similarly, individual poems quoted from a volume of poetry should be in roman, 'quoted', while the title of the volume itself should be in italic. Names of pictures should be in roman, 'quoted'. Names of ships to be in italic; prefixes and the possessive 's' to be in roman, e.g.: The *Aquitania*'s hull.

In music, song titles are to be roman, 'quoted', and subject-titles to be italic as, for example, Verdi's *Falstaff*, Bizet's *Carmen*, *but* Bach's Mass in B minor, 'Waldstein' Sonata, Beethoven's Fifth Symphony.

Musical terms of expression should be in roman, but in italics for their contracted form: forte, piano, but *f*, *p*, *pp*, *mf*, etc.

DIVISION OF WORDS

Close spacing involves more frequent division of words, but the following rules should be applied as far as possible. Divide after a vowel, turning over the consonant. In present participles take over -ing, as divid-ing, rest-ing. When two consonants come together put the hyphen between them, as haemor-rhage, forget-ting, trick-ling. The terminations -tion, -cious, -cial may be taken over entire, but must not themselves be divided. The part of the word at the end of a line should suggest the remainder of the word: starva-tion, *not* star-vation. A broken word should not be allowed to end a page, neither should it end the last full line of a paragraph if it is at all possible to avoid it, nor should a page start with a short line.

Words derived from Latin and Greek should be divided so that each component part retains its complete form. For example: philo-sophy, archaeo-logy, geo-graphy, manu-script, litho-graphy, laryngo-logy, atmo-sphere.

FIGURES

In descriptive matter numbers under 100 should be in words, but figures should be used when the matter consists of a sequence of stated quantities, numbers, ages, etc. Spell out indefinite numbers, e.g. 'has been done a thousand times'. Insert commas with four or more figures, 2,391. To represent an approximate date use the fewest figures possible, 1931–2, *not* 1931–32, and divide the figures by an en rule, *not* a hyphen. Dates should be set as written in descriptive matter, i.e. 'on the 20th of January 1931', but for the headings of letters, and wherever possible, set 20 January 1931. Set 250 B.C. *but* A.D. 250. In B.C. references always put the full date in a group of years, 185–122 B.C.

SETTING

Spacing should be as even as possible. Lower-case matter should be set with a thin or middle space between words rather than a thick or wider. It is not necessary to increase the space after a full stop or after ? ! ; : ' . A hair space should be inserted before the apostrophe in such phrases as that's (that is), colonel's (colonel is), in order to distinguish from the possessive case. A hair space should precede ; : ? ! and should be inserted between the opening quote and the first word. The first line of a paragraph should not be indented more than one em. Small capitals should be letter-spaced. Capital letters also should be letter-spaced when possible. All roman numerals set in capitals or small capitals should be hair-spaced. When blocks of capitals are used, the space between letters and words should be distinctly less than between lines. Avoid using short rules to divide display lines and paragraphs.

VOWEL-LIGATURES

The combinations *ae* and *oe* should each be printed as two letters in Latin, Greek, and English words: Aetna, Boeotia, larvae.

The ligatures *æ* and *œ* should, however, be used in Old English and French words: Ælfric, Cædmon, manœuvre, hors d'œuvre.

REFERENCES TO AUTHORITIES

Citation of authorities at the end of quotations should be printed as: HOMER, Odyssey, iv. 130
and at heads of chapters should usually be in contracted form:
HOR. *Carm.* II. xiv. 2. HOM. *Od.* ii. 12
Frequent citations in notes usually have the author's name in lower case, as:
Stubbs, *Constitutional History*, vol. ii, p. 74
References to the Bible: 2 Samuel xvii. 25
References to Shakespeare's plays: 2 *Henry IV*, II. i. 55

FOLIOS

Folios should be in the same size type as text and in lower-case roman numerals, starting from the half-title and recommencing in arabic figures from folio one at the first page of text or half-title of text, if any. Numbering the prelims separately in roman numerals is usually done when it is intended that the prelims should form a separate signature on their own. This is often necessary when the book has to be paged before the exact extent of the prelims is known. But there is one drawback to making a separate signature of the prelims. It will necessarily be of indeterminate length and may very well prevent an even working[1] which might have been possible if the prelims had been made an integral part of the book. And if they are such a part there seems to be no good reason for numbering them in a different style (but see page 70).

CONTENTS

The Contents should be a list of the constituent chapters of the body. The type of the Contents page must conform in face to that of the body of the book, and the heading must conform to that of the chapter.

MAKE-UP

Books should normally be made up in the following order:

Half-title	Preface
Title	Introduction
'History'[2] of book,	Corrigenda or errata (if any)[3]
with imprint	Text of book
Dedication	Appendix
Acknowledgements	Author's Notes
Contents	Glossary
List of Illustrations	Bibliography
List of Abbreviations	Index

[1] See definition under ODDMENT in Glossary.

[2] Date of publication, and dates of subsequent reprints and revised editions, often called the 'biblio'.

[3] Where a single error is mentioned, 'Corrigendum' or 'Erratum' is correct.

All the items shown on the preceding page, except the 'history' of the book, with the printer's imprint, begin generally on a right-hand page.

RUNNING HEAD-LINES

Running head-lines, when used, should begin on the second page of text, and unless instructions are given to the contrary should consist of the title of the book for left-hand pages, and the title of the chapter for the right-hand pages. Preliminary matter should be headed 'Contents', 'Introduction' etc. on both sides.

CHAPTER HEADINGS

The chapter openings should, if possible, begin a new page, but not necessarily a right-hand page. They may be dropped two or three lines and, in a long book, a little deeper still.

DROPPED INITIAL LETTERS

All dropped initial letters of words standing at the beginning of chapters or sections must appear to range with the lines of the matter which adjoins, the spacing to the right must be regulated according to the shape of the letter. In all cases initials must fit snugly.

INDENTION

The opening paragraph of an article, chapter, or other new matter should begin full out. All subsequent paragraphs should be indented one em, except where a cross-heading occurs, or where the next paragraph follows an ellipsis. In these two cases the paragraph should begin full out.

ILLUSTRATIONS

Full-page illustrations should, where possible, be printed on the right-hand side of the opening. They are then said to 'face up'.

CAPTIONS

Captions to illustrations in the text should generally be set in type two points smaller than the main body of the work.

APPENDIX

The type of the heading of the Appendix must conform to that of the chapter head, but the text may be one or two points smaller than the text of the book. Where there is more than one Appendix or Index, the plural form Appendixes or Indexes must normally be used, the alternative Appendices and Indices being reserved for medical and scientific works.

INDEX

An Index of two or more columns is to be preferred, set in type two points smaller than the text of the book. Begin each letter of the alphabet with even small capitals if an initial is not specified. Print page numbers immediately after the last word, with a comma before the figures. Divide columns by a white space, not by a rule.

FOOTNOTES

Footnotes are to be indicated by superior figures, and should be two points smaller than the text type. They must be separated from the text by a white space, not by a rule. Notes to a short page must be brought down to the foot of the page and not 'skied'. If it is found necessary to break a footnote, the portion turned over takes precedence over other footnotes on that page.

MARKS USED IN THE CORRECTION OF PROOFS

caps. ⌐—Every period of civilisation which forms a complete and con-   *z/*
sistent whole, manifests itself not only in political life, in
religion, art and science, but also sets its characteristic stamp
on social life. Thus the Middle ages had their courtly and aristocratic manners and etiquette, differing but little in the various
countries of Europe, as well as their peculiar forms of middle-
class life. Italian customs at the time of the Renaissance offer in
these respects the sharpest contrast Mediævalism. The foundation
on which they rest is wholly different. Social intercourse in its
its highest and most perfect form now ignored all distinctions
of caste, and was based simply on the existence of an educated class
as we now understand the word. Birth and origin were without
influence, unless combined with leisure and inherited wealth.
Yet this assertion must not be taken in an absolute and unqualified sense, since mediæval Distinctions still sometimes made

CORRECTED

EVERY period of civilization which forms a complete and consistent whole, manifests itself not only in political life, in religion,
art and science, but also sets its characteristic stamp on social life.
Thus the Middle Ages had their courtly and aristocratic manners
and etiquette, differing but little in the various countries of Europe,
as well as their peculiar forms of middle-class life.

Italian customs at the time of the Renaissance offer in these
respects the sharpest contrast to Mediævalism. The foundation on
which they rest is wholly different. Social intercourse in its highest
and most perfect form now ignored all distinctions of caste, and
was based simply on the existence of an educated class as we now
understand the word. Birth and origin were without influence,
unless combined with leisure and inherited wealth. Yet this
assertion must not be taken in an absolute and unqualified sense,
since mediæval distinctions still sometimes made themselves felt

CHOOSING THE TYPE FACE

'TYPE, the voice of the printed page, can be legible and dull, or legible and fascinating, according to its design and treatment. In other words, what the booklover calls readability is not a synonym for what the optician calls legibility.'[1] There are, in fact, aesthetic considerations which prompt people to prefer one type rather than another, considerations closely linked with the emotions and difficult to define precisely. Likewise, aesthetics are a dominant factor for those who prefer a classic to be reprinted in a type indicative of its own 'period', and similar to this is the effort to produce 'atmosphere' aided by the choice of type face. Again, illustrated books raise their own aesthetic problems in the choice of a type. But to an equal degree it can be claimed that the choice of type face is dependent on such practical considerations as the kind of book, the particular public to which the book must appeal, its length, its size, the type area to be decided, the type size and finally the leading. The paper to be used is always a factor to be taken into consideration. Owing to the great diversity of authors' MSS. it is obviously impossible to suggest a printer's reaction to every occasion, but, for our own purpose, we can examine the deservedly popular book faces in current use shown on pages 14–17, and try to ascertain the reasons why, under certain conditions, we would choose one type face rather than another.

Some, or all, of these type faces have had the support of our most eminent practitioners because of their high degree of legibility and the grace of their letter forms. They are, in their way, a cross-section of our typographical world, in that we have represented types revived from an earlier age, new types and types which are a compromise between the old and the new. The twenty-three examples show all the sizes in 12 pt., a size which,

[1] Paul Beaujon: *The Monotype Recorder*, Vol. 32, No. 1. 1933.

on the average, is the test of the norm of a book face. We are aware that a type viewed as a specimen may be one thing, whilst a type in use may somehow look different. How a type is *used* (measure, spacing, leading, paper on which it is printed, inking) is of primary importance. Leading, for instance, has the optical effect of altering the colour[1] values of the type on the printed page: the greater the amount of leading the lighter in colour a type appears. The colour value of type is also affected by the kind of paper on which type is printed. Again, some types such as Caslon, Garamond and Perpetua attain their finest flowering in their larger sizes, whilst Fournier, Plantin and Imprint are, for various reasons, more successful in their smaller sizes.

Our twenty-three type faces shown on pages 14–17, when compared, show several important differences concerning:

(*a*) Width of letters
(*b*) Size of the type face on the type body
(*c*) Shading of the thick strokes
(*d*) Length of ascenders and descenders
(*e*) Size of capital letters
(*f*) General weight and colour of the type face.

These differences, as we shall see, have a practical importance of their own apart from any aesthetic considerations.

(*a*) WIDTH OF LETTERS

Although the type faces shown on pages 14–17 are all set in 12 pt., nevertheless the length of the alphabet varies in both capitals and lower-case. This variation affects the number of words that can conveniently be printed on a page, exclusive of any necessity, or otherwise, of leading. The roman lower-case letters of Scotch and Baskerville, for instance, are wide and generous, whilst, at the other extreme, Fournier and Bembo occupy considerably less width. This obvious difference in width of letters,

[1] A black impression can range from jet black to grey; see page 31.

TYPE FACES
FOR TEXT COMPOSITION
showing alphabet widths

★ *Monotype*   † *Linotype*   § *Intertype*

★BASKERVILLE 169

ABCDEFGHIJKLMNOPQRSTUVWXYZ
abcdefghijklmnopqrstuvwxyz 1234567890
ABCDEFGHIJKLMNOPQRSTUVWXYZ
abcdefghijklmnopqrstuvwxyz 1234567890

★BELL 341

ABCDEFGHIJKLMNOPQRSTUVWXYZ
abcdefghijklmnopqrstuvwxyz 1234567890
ABCDEFGHIJKLMNOPQRSTUVWXYZ
abcdefghijklmnopqrstuvwxyz 1234567890

★BEMBO

ABCDEFGHIJKLMNOPQRSTUVWXYZ
abcdefghijklmnopqrstuvwxyz 1234567890
ABCDEFGHIJKLMNOPQRSTUVWXYZ
abcdefghijklmnopqrstuvwxyz 1234567890

§BODONI

ABCDEFGHIJKLMNOPQRSTUVWXYZ
abcdefghijklmnopqrstuvwxyz 1234567890
ABCDEFGHIJKLMNOPQRSTUVWXYZ
abcdefghijklmnopqrstuvwxyz 1234567890

★BULMER 469

ABCDEFGHIJKLMNOPQRSTUVWXYZ
abcdefghijklmnopqrstuvwxyz 1234567890
ABCDEFGHIJKLMNOPQRSTUVWXYZ
abcdefghijklmnopqrstuvwxyz 1234567890

14

† CALEDONIA

ABCDEFGHIJKLMNOPQRSTUVWXYZ
abcdefghijklmnopqrstuvwxyz 1234567890
ABCDEFGHIJKLMNOPQRSTUVWXYZ
abcdefghijklmnopqrstuvwxyz 1234567890

★ CENTAUR 252

ABCDEFGHIJKLMNOPQRSTUVWXYZ
abcdefghijklmnopqrstuvwxyz 1234567890
ABCDEFGHIJKLMNOPQRSTUVWXYZ
abcdefghijklmnopqrstuvwxyz 1234567890

§ CORNELL

ABCDEFGHIJKLMNOPQRSTUVWXYZ
abcdefghijklmnopqrstuvwxyz 1234567890
ABCDEFGHIJKLMNOPQRSTUVWXYZ
abcdefghijklmnopqrstuvwxyz 1234567890

★ EHRHARDT 453

ABCDEFGHIJKLMNOPQRSTUVWXYZ
abcdefghijklmnopqrstuvwxyz 1234567890
ABCDEFGHIJKLMNOPQRSTUVWXYZ
abcdefghijklmnopqrstuvwxyz 1234567890

★ FOURNIER 185

ABCDEFGHIJKLMNOPQRSTUVWXYZ
abcdefghijklmnopqrstuvwxyz 1234567890
ABCDEFGHIJKLMNOPQRSTUVWXYZ
abcdefghijklmnopqrstuvwxyz 1234567890

★ GARAMOND 156

ABCDEFGHIJKLMNOPQRSTUVWXYZ
abcdefghijklmnopqrstuvwxyz 1234567890
ABCDEFGHIJKLMNOPQRSTUVWXYZ
abcdefghijklmnopqrstuvwxyz 1234567890

† GEORGIAN

ABCDEFGHIJKLMNOPQRSTUVWXYZ
abcdefghijklmnopqrstuvwxyz 1234567890
ABCDEFGHIJKLMNOPQRSTUVWXYZ
abcdefghijklmnopqrstuvwxyz 1234567890

† GRANJON

ABCDEFGHIJKLMNOPQRSTUVWXYZ
abcdefghijklmnopqrstuvwxyz 1234567890
ABCDEFGHIJKLMNOPQRSTUVWXYZ
abcdefghijklmnopqrstuvwxyz 1234567890

*IMPRINT 101

ABCDEFGHIJKLMNOPQRSTUVWXYZ
abcdefghijklmnopqrstuvwxyz 1234567890
ABCDEFGHIJKLMNOPQRSTUVWXYZ
abcdefghijklmnopqrstuvwxyz 1234567890

† JULIANA

ABCDEFGHIJKLMNOPQRSTUVWXYZ
abcdefghijklmnopqrstuvwxyz 1234567890
ABCDEFGHIJKLMNOPQRSTUVWXYZ
abcdefghijklmnopqrstuvwxyz 1234567890

*PERPETUA 239

ABCDEFGHIJKLMNOPQRSTUVWXYZ
abcdefghijklmnopqrstuvwxyz 1234567890
ABCDEFGHIJKLMNOPQRSTUVWXYZ
abcdefghijklmnopqrstuvwxyz 1234567890

† PILGRIM

ABCDEFGHIJKLMNOPQRSTUVWXYZ
abcdefghijklmnopqrstuvwxyz 1234567890
ABCDEFGHIJKLMNOPQRSTUVWXYZ
abcdefghijklmnopqrstuvwxyz 1234567890

*PLANTIN 110

ABCDEFGHIJKLMNOPQRSTUVWXYZ
abcdefghijklmnopqrstuvwxyz 1234567890
ABCDEFGHIJKLMNOPQRSTUVWXYZ
abcdefghijklmnopqrstuvwxyz 1234567890

*POLIPHILUS 170 & BLADO ITALIC 119

ABCDEFGHIJKLMNOPQRSTUVWXYZ
abcdefghijklmnopqrstuvwxyz 1234567890
ABCDEFGHIJKLMNOPQRSTUVWXYZ
abcdefghijklmnopqrstuvwxyz 1234567890

*SCOTCH ROMAN 46

ABCDEFGHIJKLMNOPQRSTUVWXYZ
abcdefghijklmnopqrstuvwxyz 1234567890
ABCDEFGHIJKLMNOPQRSTUVWXYZ
abcdefghijklmnopqrstuvwxyz

*TIMES 327 with long descenders.

ABCDEFGHIJKLMNOPQRSTUVWXYZ
abcdefghijklmnopqrstuvwxyz 1234567890
ABCDEFGHIJKLMNOPQRSTUVWXYZ
abcdefghijklmnopqrstuvwxyz 1234567890

*VAN DIJCK 203

ABCDEFGHIJKLMNOPQRSTUVWXYZ
abcdefghijklmnopqrstuvwxyz 1234567890
ABCDEFGHIJKLMNOPQRSTUVWXYZ
abcdefghijklmnopqrstuvwxyz 1234567890

*WALBAUM 374

ABCDEFGHIJKLMNOPQRSTUVWXYZ
abcdefghijklmnopqrstuvwxyz 1234567890
ABCDEFGHIJKLMNOPQRSTUVWXYZ
abcdefghijklmnopqrstuvwxyz 1234567890

or 'set' as it is called in the trade, will frequently be an important consideration in choosing a type for a short book on the one hand, or a very long book on the other, and types that are width-saving have obvious attractions for books set in double column. But this is, after all, only one of several considerations in choosing a type: there are other factors which we must examine and which, in their turn, contribute their influence to our choice.

(b) SIZE OF THE TYPE FACE ON THE TYPE BODY

A further examination of the types on pages 14–17 shows very considerable differences in the size of the actual type face on the 12-pt. body. These differences become even more obvious the larger the type sizes become. If a page of each of these twenty-three type faces were set solid, the size of the actual face on the 12-pt. body would not affect the number of words per square inch except in so far as the 'set' of the face is wide or narrow. But the size of the type face on the body does give a pointer to the body size that might be chosen with a view to the maximum legibility in combination with the degree of leading compatible with an agreeable page of type. Plantin and Times, for instance, are, in relation to others, so large on their bodies that whilst 12 pt. is the norm for almost all the types exhibited, the equivalent could well be 11 pt. in their case (pages 23–4). This 'largeness' on the body is measured first in terms of the height of the non-ascending and non-descending lower-case letters, e.g. x (hence the term 'x-height'), and secondly, the width of the m (which determines the 'set'). A type like Times may thus be described as large on the body but of narrow set.

Types that are, or tend to be, large on their bodies benefit from being set leaded in all sizes except when the measure is narrow. This helps legibility and enhances any aesthetic appeal a type may possess, notably Times, Baskerville, Bodoni, Garamond, Imprint, Plantin, and Scotch.

It soon became obvious that the future of the Bill depended upon the support of influential members such as John Bright, who would not be satisfied unless it contained clauses providing for a poll of the ratepayers affected prior to local adoptions. Grave suspicion of the activities of town councils was expressed during the debate, a suspicion which students of British local government during the first part of the nineteenth century will not find difficult to comprehend. Ewart promised to 'give his careful consideration' to 'objections aroused during the debate'

12 pt. Baskerville ★

It soon became obvious that the future of the Bill depended upon the support of influential members such as John Bright, who would not be satisfied unless it contained clauses providing for a poll of the ratepayers affected prior to local adoptions. Grave suspicion of the activities of town councils was expressed during the debate, a suspicion which students of British local government during the first part of the nineteenth century will not find difficult to comprehend. Ewart promised to 'give his careful consideration' to 'objections aroused during the debate' and to 'endeavour if possible to meet them'. Even so the second reading was only carried

12 pt. Bembo ★

Bright, who would not be satisfied unless it contained clauses providing for a poll of the ratepayers affected prior to local adoptions. Grave suspicion of the activities of town councils was expressed during the debate, a suspicion which students of British local government during the first part of the nineteenth century will not find difficult to comprehend. Ewart promised to 'give his careful consideration' to 'objections aroused during the debate' and to 'endeavour if possible to meet them'. Even so the second reading was only carried by the narrow majority of seventeen (Ayes

12 pt. Bodoni §

upon the support of influential members such as John Bright, who would not be satisfied unless it contained clauses providing for a poll of the ratepayers affected prior to local adoptions. Grave suspicion of the activities of town councils was expressed during the debate, a suspicion which students of British local government during the first part of the nineteenth century will not find difficult to comprehend. Ewart promised to 'give his careful consideration' to 'objections aroused during the debate' and to 'endeavour if possible to meet them'. Even so the second reading was only carried by

12 pt. Bulmer *

It soon became obvious that the future of the Bill depended upon the support of influential members such as John Bright, who would not be satisfied unless it contained clauses providing for a poll of the ratepayers affected prior to local adoptions. Grave suspicion of the activities of town councils was expressed during the debate, a suspicion which students of British local government during the first part of the nineteenth century will not find difficult to comprehend. Ewart promised to 'give his careful consideration' to 'objections aroused during the debate' and to 'endeavour if possible to meet them'. Even

11 on 12 pt. Caledonia † with long descenders

It soon became obvious that the future of the Bill depended upon the support of influential members such as John Bright, who would not be satisfied unless it contained clauses providing for a poll of the ratepayers affected prior to local adoptions. Grave suspicion of the activities of town councils was expressed during the debate, a suspicion which students of British local government during the first part of the nineteenth century will not find difficult to comprehend. Ewart promised to 'give his careful consideration' to 'objections aroused during the debate' and to 'endeavour if possible to meet them'. Even

12 pt. Caslon *

Bright, who would not be satisfied unless it contained clauses providing for a poll of the ratepayers affected prior to local adoptions. Grave suspicion of the activities of town councils was expressed during the debate, a suspicion which students of British local government during the first part of the nineteenth century will not find difficult to comprehend. Ewart promised to 'give his careful consideration' to 'objections aroused during the debate' and to 'endeavour if possible to meet them'. Even so the second reading was only carried by the narrow majority of seventeen

12 pt. Cornell §

It soon became obvious that the future of the Bill depended upon the support of influential members such as John Bright, who would not be satisfied unless it contained clauses providing for a poll of the ratepayers affected prior to local adoptions. Grave suspicion of the activities of town councils was expressed during the debate, a suspicion which students of British local government during the first part of the nineteenth century will not find difficult to comprehend. Ewart promised to 'give his careful consideration' to 'objections aroused during the debate' and to 'endeavour if possible to meet them'. Even

12 pt. Ehrhardt *

It soon became obvious that the future of the Bill depended upon the support of influential members such as John Bright, who would not be satisfied unless it contained clauses providing for a poll of the ratepayers affected prior to local adoptions. Grave suspicion of the activities of town councils was expressed during the debate, a suspicion which students of British local government during the first part of the nineteenth century will not find difficult to comprehend. Ewart promised to 'give his careful consideration' to 'objections aroused during the debate' and to 'endeavour if possible to

12 pt. Garamond *

It soon became obvious that the future of the Bill depended upon the support of influential members such as John Bright, who would not be satisfied unless it contained clauses providing for a poll of the ratepayers affected prior to local adoptions. Grave suspicion of the activities of town councils was expressed during the debate, a suspicion which students of British local government during the first part of the nineteenth century will not find difficult to comprehend. Ewart promised to 'give his careful consideration' to 'objections aroused during the debate' and to 'endeavour if possible to

12 pt. Georgian †

It soon became obvious that the future of the Bill depended upon the support of influential members such as John Bright, who would not be satisfied unless it contained clauses providing for a poll of the ratepayers affected prior to local adoptions. Grave suspicion of the activities of town councils was expressed during the debate, a suspicion which students of British local government during the first part of the nineteenth century will not find difficult to comprehend. Ewart promised to 'give his careful consideration' to 'objections aroused during the debate' and to 'endeavour if possible to meet them'. Even so the second reading

12 pt. Granjon †

depended upon the support of influential members such as John Bright, who would not be satisfied unless it contained clauses providing for a poll of the ratepayers affected prior to local adoptions. Grave suspicion of the activities of town councils was expressed during the debate, a suspicion which students of British local government during the first part of the nineteenth century will not find difficult to comprehend. Ewart promised to 'give his careful consideration' to 'objections aroused during the debate' and to 'endeavour if possible to meet them'. Even so the second reading was

12 pt. Imprint *

22

It soon became obvious that the future of the Bill depended upon
the support of influential members such as John Bright, who
would not be satisfied unless it contained clauses providing for a
poll of the ratepayers affected prior to local adoptions. Grave suspicion of the activities of town councils was expressed during the
debate, a suspicion which students of British local government
during the first part of the nineteenth century will not find difficult to comprehend. Ewart promised to 'give his careful consideration' to 'objections aroused during the debate' and to 'endeavour
if possible to meet them'. Even so the second reading was only

11 on 12 pt. Juliana † with long descenders

depended upon the support of influential members such
as John Bright, who would not be satisfied unless it contained clauses providing for a poll of the ratepayers affected
prior to local adoptions. Grave suspicion of the activities
of town councils was expressed during the debate, a suspicion which students of British local government during
the first part of the nineteenth century will not find difficult to comprehend. Ewart promised to 'give his careful
consideration' to 'objections aroused during the debate'
and to 'endeavour if possible to meet them'. Even so the

12 pt. Plantin *

such as John Bright, who would not be satisfied unless
it contained clauses providing for a poll of the ratepayers affected prior to local adoptions. Grave suspicion of the activities of town councils was expressed
during the debate, a suspicion which students of
British local government during the first part of the
nineteenth century will not find difficult to comprehend. Ewart promised to 'give his careful consideration' to 'objections aroused during the debate' and to
'endeavour if possible to meet them'. Even so the

`12 pt. Scotch Roman *

23

It soon became obvious that the future of the Bill depended upon the support of influential members such as John Bright, who would not be satisfied unless it contained clauses providing for a poll of the ratepayers affected prior to local adoptions. Grave suspicion of the activities of town councils was expressed during the debate, a suspicion which students of British local government during the first part of the nineteenth century will not find difficult to comprehend. Ewart promised to 'give his careful consideration' to 'objections aroused during the debate' and to 'endeavour if possible to meet them'. Even so the second reading

11 on 12 pt. Times ★ with long descenders

the support of influential members such as John Bright, who would not be satisfied unless it contained clauses providing for a poll of the ratepayers affected prior to local adoptions. Grave suspicion of the activities of town councils was expressed during the debate, a suspicion which students of British local government during the first part of the nineteenth century will not find difficult to comprehend. Ewart promised to 'give his careful consideration' to 'objections aroused during the debate' and to 'endeavour if possible to meet them'. Even so the second reading was only carried by the narrow majority of seventeen (Ayes 118, Noes 101). L. W. Buck

11 on 12 pt. Van Dijck ★

the support of influential members such as John Bright, who would not be satisfied unless it contained clauses providing for a poll of the ratepayers affected prior to local adoptions. Grave suspicion of the activities of town councils was expressed during the debate, a suspicion which students of British local government during the first part of the nineteenth century will not find difficult to comprehend. Ewart promised to 'give his careful consideration' to 'objections aroused during the debate' and to 'endeavour if possible to

12 on 13 pt. Walbaum ★

24

8 pt. # POETRY IS

2 pt. # INDEED SOME

5 pt. # THING DIVINE. IT

9 pt. # IS AT ONCE THE CE

4 pt. NTRE AND CIRCUMFERE

8 pt. NCE OF KNOWLEDGE; IT IS THAT

4 pt. WHICH COMPREHENDS ALL SCIENCE, AND
THAT TO WHICH ALL SCIENCE MUST BE

2 pt. REFERRED. . . . IT IS THE PERFECT AND CONSU
MMATE SURFACE AND BLOOM OF ALL THINGS;

pt. IT IS AS THE ODOUR AND THE COLOUR OF THE
ROSE TO THE TEXTURE OF THE ELEMENTS WHICH

9 pt. COMPOSE IT, AS THE FORM AND SPLENDOUR OF UNFA
DED BEAUTY TO THE SECRETS OF ANATOMY AND COR

pt. RUPTION. WHAT WERE VIRTUE, LOVE, PATRIOTISM, FRIEND
SHIP—WHAT WERE THE SCENERY OF THIS BEAUTIFUL UNI

8 pt. VERSE WHICH WE INHABIT; WHAT WERE OUR CONSOLATIONS ON
THIS SIDE OF THE GRAVE—AND WHAT WERE OUR ASPIRATIONS

Fournier: small on its body, 8 pt.–48 pt. roman capitals.

beyond it, if poetry did not ascend to bring 18 p
light and fire from those eternal regions
where the owl-winged faculty of calculation

dare not ever soar? Poetry is not like reasoning, a power 14 p
to be exerted according to the determination of the will.
A man cannot say, "I will compose poetry". The greatest
poet even cannot say it; for the mind in creation is as a

fading coal, which some invisible influence, like an inconstant 12 p
wind, awakens to transitory brightness; this power arises from
within, like the colour of a flower which fades and changes as it is
developed, and the conscious portions of our natures are unpro-
phetic either of its approach or its departure. . . . Poetry is the
record of the best and happiest moments of the happiest and best

minds. We are aware of evanescent visitations of thought and feeling 11p
sometimes associated with place or person, sometimes regarding our
own mind alone, and always arising unforeseen and departing unbid-
den, but elevating and delightful beyond all expression: so that even in
the desire and regret they leave, there cannot but be pleasure, partici-
pating as it does in the nature of its object. It is as it were the interpene-

tration of a diviner nature through our own; but its footsteps are like those of 10 p
a wind over the sea, which the coming calm erases, and whose traces remain
only, as on the wrinkled sand which paves it. These and corresponding conditions of being are experienced principally by those of the most delicate
sensibility and the most enlarged imagination; and the state of mind produced
by them is at war with every base desire. The enthusiasm of virtue, love,

9 pt. they last, self appears as what it is, an | the enchanted chord, and reanimate, in 8 p
atom to a universe. Poets are not only those who have ever experienced these
subject to these experiences as spirits of emotions, the sleeping, the cold, the buried
the most refined organization, but they image of the past. Poetry thus makes im-
can colour all that they combine with mortal all that is best and most beautiful in
the evanescent hues of this ethereal the world; it arrests the vanishing appari-
world; a word, a trait in the representa- tions which haunt the interlunations of life,
tion of a scene or a passion, will touch and veiling them, or in language or in form,
sends them forth among mankind.

Fournier: small on its body, 8 pt.–18 pt. lower case roman.

pt. # THE MOST

pt. # UNFAILING H

pt. # ERALD, COMPANI

pt. # ON, & FOLLOWER OF

pt. # THE WAKENING OF A GREAT

pt. PEOPLE TO WORK A BENEFICIAL CHANGE
IN OPINION OR INSTITUTION, IS POETRY.

pt. AT SUCH PERIODS THERE IS AN ACCUMULA
TION OF THE POWER OF COMMUNICATING

pt. AND RECEIVING INTENSE AND IMPASSIONED CON
CEPTIONS RESPECTING MAN AND NATURE. THE

pt. PERSONS IN WHOM THIS POWER RESIDES MAY OFTEN,
AS FAR AS REGARDS MANY PORTIONS OF THEIR NA

pt. TURE, HAVE LITTLE APPARENT CORRESPONDENCE WITH
THAT SPIRIT OF GOOD OF WHICH THEY ARE THE MINIS

pt. TERS. BUT EVEN WHILST THEY DENY AND ABJURE, THEY ARE
YET COMPELLED TO SERVE THE POWER WHICH IS SEATED ON

Times Roman: large on its body, 8 pt.–48 pt. roman capitals.

27

the throne of their own soul. It is 18 p

impossible to read the compositions

of the most celebrated writers of the

present day without being startled with the electric 14 p
life which burns within their words. They measure
the circumference and sound the depths of human
nature with a comprehensive and all-penetrating

spirit, and they are themselves perhaps the most sin- 12 p
cerely astonished at its manifestations; for it is less their
spirit than the spirit of the age. Poets are the hierophants
of an unapprehended inspiration; the mirrors of the
gigantic shadows which futurity casts upon the present;

the words which express what they understand not; the trumpets 11 p
which sing to battle, and feel not what they inspire; the influence
which is moved not, but moves. Poets are the unacknowledged
legislators of the world. Time has thrown its purple shadow
athwart this scene, and no more is visible than the broad and
everlasting character of human strength and genius, that pledge

of all that is to be admirable and lovely in ages yet to come. Solemn 10 p
Temples, where the senate of the world assembled, palaces, triumphal
arches, and cloud-surrounded columns, loaded with the sculptured
annals of conquest and domination—what actions and deliberations
have they been destined to enclose and commemorate? Superstitious
rites, which in their mildest form, outrage reason, and obscure the

9 pt. devastation, and misrule, and servi-   chariot, exhibiting, as titles to renown, 8 pt
tude; and lastly, these schemes   the labour of ages, and the admired
brought to their tremendous con-   creations of genius, overthrown by the
summations, and a human being   brutal force, which was placed as a
returning in the midst of festival and   sword within his hand, and—contem-
solemn joy, with thousands and   plation fearful and abhorred!—he him-
thousands of his enslaved and deso-   **self, a being capable of the gentlest and**
lated species chained behind his   **best emotions, inspired with the belief**
    that he has done a virtuous deed!

Times Roman: large on its body, 8 pt.–18 pt. lower case roman.
Times Bold is also shown and is of the same width as Times Roman

28

A full moon around the time of the beginning of autumn is called a harvest moon. At this time the moon may rise only about fifteen minutes later each night instead of the usual fifty minutes. The phrase had its beginnings in early England and is so called because farmers can harvest their crops late into the evening by the light of the full moon, and the moon will shine for many nights.

In order to understand why there is a harvest moon, we must have some knowledge of the meaning of culmination. Directly over your head, and running from north to south, is the imaginary line called your meridian. Whenever a celestial object crosses that meridian at any point, we say that it culminates; the event is a culmination.

The moon moves rapidly towards the east in its passage around the earth. Because of this rapid motion, the moon cul-

A full moon around the time of the beginning of autumn is called a harvest moon. At this time the moon may rise only about fifteen minutes later each night instead of the usual fifty minutes. The phrase had its beginnings in early England and is so called because farmers can harvest their crops late into the evening by the light of the full moon, and the moon will shine for many nights.

In order to understand why there is a harvest moon, we must have some knowledge of the meaning of culmination. Directly over your head, and running from north to south, is the imaginary line called your meridian. Whenever a celestial object crosses that meridian at any point, we say that it culminates; the event is a culmination.

The moon moves rapidly towards the east in its passage around the earth. Because of this rapid motion, the moon culminates—

At the top of the page are some lines of film-set Plantin enlarged photographically from 8 pt. to approximately 11 pt. Below is 11 on 13 pt. Plantin conventionally set for comparison. The greater width and lighter colour of the film version will be at once apparent, indicating that ideally each size of type needs to be designed specially, not enlarged or reduced from a prototype.

(c) SHADING OF THE THICK STROKES

One of the characteristics of a type face is the contrast of the thick and thin strokes; this has a practical significance. In those types where the contrast is most pronounced, the shading of the rounded strokes might be described as vertical, notably in Bodoni, Scotch and Walbaum. We submit that types with heavy vertical shading should always be set leaded in all sizes, otherwise the lines, if set solid, would have a dazzling effect to the eyes. Baskerville stands midway between vertical and rounded shading and is enhanced by being set leaded. Bembo, Caslon, Garamond, Perpetua, and Centaur are examples of rounded and more gradual shading, and as Bembo, Caslon and Centaur are, in addition, small faces on their bodies, leading is not so essential.

Walbaum
Vertical Shading

Perpetua
Rounded Shading

(d) LENGTH OF ASCENDERS AND DESCENDERS

There are five letters in the lower-case alphabet with descenders, g, j, p, q and y, and six with ascenders, b, d, f, h, k and l. The ascending and descending letters give an automatic amount of apparent white spacing between the lines of type solidly set. When the ascenders and descenders are long, this white appears to be greater, but on the other hand, the face is, as a result, small on the body. Times is available in three versions, with short, medium and long descenders. In the version with long descenders the Times 12 pt. face is, out of necessity, on a 13-pt. body; 12 pt. Walbaum is also on a 13-pt. body. It was found expedient to put the 12 pt. Walbaum on a 13-pt. body to achieve a faithful reproduction of an old but still existing typefounders' type cast on a Didot (Continental) body. Other types, as may be seen on pages 14–17, have medium length ascenders and descenders, which show these types to appear large though remaining on a 12-pt. body.

(e) SIZE OF CAPITAL LETTERS

The capitals of most type faces are the height of the ascenders of their lower case, but in Bembo and Perpetua the capitals range lower, e.g., Thames (Bembo), Plaistow (Perpetua).

A type with capitals ranging lower than the lower-case ascenders is useful for books where there are more than the usual number of words capitalized in the text, or where whole words or even sentences occur frequently in the main text in capitals, or, again, if the book is a bibliography or a catalogue.

(f) GENERAL WEIGHT AND COLOUR OF THE TYPE FACE

Some readers have a preference for fully coloured types such as Plantin, Times, Bodoni, Scotch, Ehrhardt, and Poliphilus, whilst others find types lighter or medium in colour easier to read, e.g., Fournier and Caslon. This is generally a matter of habit or eyesight, but there is little doubt, for instance, that children prefer a black-looking type. Leading or absence of leading, together with the choice of paper, will affect the colour of a type, making colourful type faces appear lighter than they normally are, and vice versa. We shall refer to these two factors in greater detail in a section to follow.

There are, to be sure, other and more mundane factors in choosing a type face. The number of type faces a printer can stock has its limits financially, nor at any given time are the type faces he possesses necessarily complete with accented letters, bolds, and old style and modern numerals. Nor will he always have a sufficient range of sizes of every type face in his stock. For certain books therefore which demand any or all of the above-mentioned special sorts, or an abnormal number of sizes of a fount, a printer will naturally be inclined to consider what he has conveniently to hand.

4

SETTING OF THE TEXT

THE MANUSCRIPT

A PRINTER receives MSS. of endless variety and it would be impossible to suggest any one procedure to cover all occasions. A publisher of repute would, in all probability, have read carefully through the MS. before sending it to the printer. Nevertheless, as a precaution, the printer should immediately give it a cursory examination as to content. He must then assure himself, in certain categories of MS., that there is nothing which offends against either the law of libel or obscenity and, in time of war or civil commotion, that there is nothing contravening the regulations applying to censorship as imposed by the authorities.

The MS. should then be examined for punctuation and spelling, to see that the author has prepared it carefully and to note to what degree it conforms to the rule of the House. The spelling, punctuation, capitalization, etc., of an obviously careless author can well be improved by an experienced Press Reader, who should also be responsible for checking dates, titles, place-names, historical characters, etc. As De Vinne says: 'It is the belief now, as it was in the days of Moxon, the first English writer on the technics of printing, that it is the duty of the printer to supplement the negligences of the writer'.[1]

MARGINS

Margins set off and enhance the type area, just as the mount of a drawing displays a picture to its fullest advantage. Both margins and mounts are subject to the laws of proportion. The margins on the pages of a book help the eye to focus on the type area: indeed our eyes are accustomed to certain conventions, and any marked deviation means an interruption in the flow of the reading.

[1] *The Practice of Typography: Correct Composition*, by Theodore Low De Vinne. 1916.

There should be more margin at the bottom of a page than at the top, otherwise the type area has the appearance of falling out of the page. The inner margins should be less than the outer margins, as a double text-page opening strikes the eye as an entity, not as two single pages separate in themselves. Enough room should be left on the side margins for easy manipulation of the reader's thumb or finger without obscuring type matter. The bottom margin should be large enough for the comfortable placing of the reader's thumb, particularly at the period when the last lines of the page are being read. Good margins are an aid to legibility (see page 34), and, apart from the above considerations, the larger amount of margin on sides, head and tail allows for subsequent cutting and rebinding without injury to the type area. Ample margins also give room to the reader for annotation.

When a book is printed with hanging shoulder (marginal) notes to the text, they must be considered, typographically, as part of the type area of the text, and the surrounding margin should consequently make allowance for these notes (page 35).

In pocket editions, where the text has to be condensed into a small area, margins are inevitably slight. The pages are therefore imposed a little above the optical centre of the page, whilst the merely nominal inner and side margins will be equal (page 35).

When type face, type size and margins have been chosen provisionally, a cast-off can be made of the MS., which will be shown to make a book of x pages.

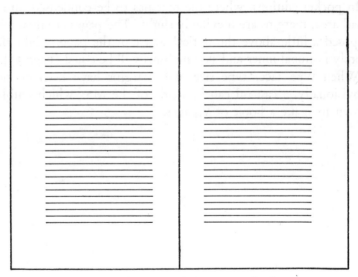

Suggested margins for a quarto book.

Suggested margins for an octavo book.

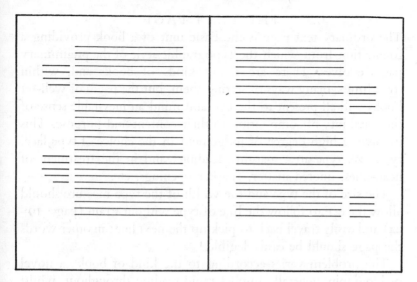

Quarto book, showing margins allowing for hanging shoulder notes.

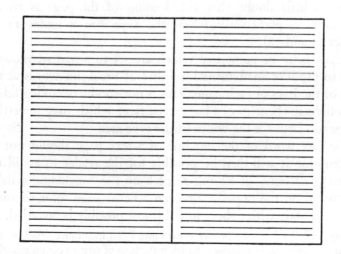

Pocket edition, with slight margins.

THE TEXT PAGE

The ordinary text page is the basic unit of a book providing a foundation from which the typographic style of the preliminary pages evolves. There are many kinds of books and, within strict limits, many ways of setting them, but the pages of well-set books will all present to the eye and mind an inevitable sense of the suitability of composition to their content and purpose. This involves a high degree of judgement in the choice of type face, type size, type area, margins, leading; and in the treatment of head-lines, quoted matter, chapter openings, etc.

The size of the type and the width of the type measure should allow the eye to follow the line of type without strain (pages 19–24) and easily travel back to pick up the next line; in other words the page should be easily legible.[1]

The problem varies according to the kind of book: a novel or biography generally implies rapid reading throughout, whilst in poetry the tempo would be slower. Works of reference and dictionaries, on the other hand, are read only for specific entries. There is little doubt that the leading of the page is an aid to legibility, particularly when the type size is under 12 pt. (pages 37 and 38).

Types large in point size which are set to a narrow measure tend to produce an abnormal number of breaks in words at the ends of the lines of each page. This is not conducive to legibility, and offsets the benefits of a large type face, which may nevertheless be too large for the width of the type area.

The last word of the last line of a text page should not be broken, for it will then be possible for the reader to avoid the irritating necessity of having to pick up the concluding syllable of a word on the opposite or even a verso page. Nor should a page ever start with a short line if it can possibly be avoided.

[1] 'By legibility I mean a proper observance in all its infinite details of that principle of order and convention which is the basis of written communication. Printing is the vehicle: legibility is the well-greased bearing that allows the wheels of sense to revolve without squealing.'—Francis Meynell, *The Monotype Recorder*, Vol. 32. No. 3. 1933.

will seek to come at even hand, by depressing another's fortune. A man that is busy and inquisitive is commonly envious; for to know much of other men's matters cannot be because all that ado may concern his own estate; therefore it must needs be that he taketh a kind of play-pleasure in looking upon the fortunes of others; neither can he that mindeth but his own business find much matter for envy; for envy is a gadding passion, and walketh the streets, and doth not keep home: 'Non est curiosus, quin idem sit malevolus'. Men of noble birth are noted to be envious towards new men when they rise: for the distance is

8 pt. Imprint solid.

altered; and it is like a deceit of the eye, that when others come on they think themselves go back. Deformed persons and eunuchs, and old men and bastards, are envious; for he that cannot possibly mend his own case, will do what he can to impair another's; except these defects light upon a very brave and heroical nature, which thinketh to make his natural wants part of his honour; in that it should be said, 'That an eunuch, or a lame man, did such great matters'; affecting the honour of a miracle: as it was in Narses the eunuch, and Agesilaus and Tamerlane, that were lame men. The same is the case of men who rise after

8 on 9 pt. Imprint.

calamities and misfortunes; for they are as men fallen out with the times, and think other men's harms a redemption of their own sufferings. They that desire to excel in too many matters, out of levity and vain glory, are ever envious, for they cannot want work—it being impossible but many, in some one of those things, should surpass them; which was the character of Adrian the emperor, that mortally envied poets and painters, and artificers in works wherein he had a vein to excel. Lastly, near kinsfolks and fellows in office, and those that are bred together, are more apt to envy their equals when they are raised; for it doth

8 on 10 pt. Imprint.

upbraid unto them their own fortunes, and pointeth at them, and cometh oftener into their remembrance, and incurreth likewise more into the note of others; and envy ever redoubleth from speech and fame. Cain's envy was the more vile and malignant towards his brother Abel, because, when his sacrifice was better accepted, there was nobody to look on. Thus much for those that are apt to envy. Concerning those that are more or less subject to envy. First, persons of eminent virtue, when they are advanced, are less envied, for their fortune seemeth but due unto them: and no man envieth the payment of a debt, but rewards and liberality rather. Again, envy is ever joined with the comparing of a man's self;

8 on 11 pt. Imprint.

Imprint set solid and leaded.

There be none of the affections which have been noted to fascinate or bewitch, but love and envy; they both have vehement wishes, they frame themselves readily into imagination and suggestions, and they come easily into the eye, especially upon the presence of the objects, which are the points that conduce to fascination, if any such thing there

11 pt. Baskerville solid.

be. We see, likewise, the Scripture calleth envy an evil eye, and the astrologers call the evil influences of the stars evil aspects, so that still there seemeth to be acknowledged, in the act of envy, an ejaculation or irradiation of the eye; nay, some have been so curious as to note, that the times when the stroke or percussion of an envious eye doth most hurt, are when the

11 on 12 pt. Baskerville.

party envied is beheld in glory or triumph, for that sets an edge upon envy; and besides, at such times, the spirits of the person envied do come forth most into the outward parts, and so meet the blow. But, leaving these curiosities (though not unworthy to be thought on in fit place), we will handle what persons are apt to envy others; what persons are most subject

11 on 13 pt. Baskerville.

to be envied themselves; and what is the difference between public and private envy. A man that hath no virtue in himself ever envieth virtue in others—for men's minds will either feed upon their own good, or upon others' evil; and who wanteth the one will prey upon the other; and whoso is out of hope to attain another's virtue, will seek to come at even hand, by depressing another's fortune. A man that is busy and inquisitive

11 on 14 pt. Baskerville.

Baskerville set solid and leaded.

38

A life of action and danger moderates the dread of death. It not only gives us fortitude to bear pain, but teaches us at every step the precarious tenure on which we hold our present being. Sedentary and studious men are the most apprehensive on this score. Dr. Johnson was an instance in point. A few years seemed to him soon over, compared with those sweeping contemplations on time and infinity with which he had been used to pose himself. In the *still-life* of a man of letters, there was no obvious reason for a change. He might sit in an arm-chair and pour out cups of tea to all eternity. Would it had been possible for him to do so! The most rational cure after all for the inordinate fear of death is to set a just value on life. If we merely wish to continue on the scene to indulge our headstrong humours and tormenting passions, we had better

(*a*) Spacing too wide after a full point, resulting in rivers of obtrusive white. There is a distressing amount of space between words compared with space between lines.

A life of action and danger moderates the dread of death. It not only gives us fortitude to bear pain, but teaches us at every step the precarious tenure on which we hold our present being. Sedentary and studious men are the most apprehensive on this score. Dr. Johnson was an instance in point. A few years seemed to him soon over, compared with those sweeping contemplations on time and infinity with which he had been used to pose himself. In the *still-life* of a man of letters, there was no obvious reason for a change. He might sit in an arm-chair and pour out cups of tea to all eternity. Would it had been possible for him to do so! The most rational cure after all for the inordinate fear of death is to set a just value on life. If we merely wish to continue on the scene to indulge our headstrong humours and tormenting passions, we had better begone at once: and if we only cherish a fondness for existence according to the good

(*b*) The same as above set more closely with spacing as even as possible.

Examples of wide and close setting.

Spacing between words should be as even as possible (page 39) if it is desired to avoid rivers of white straggling down the page; and, indeed, even spacing makes an important contribution towards an harmonious-looking page.

Both well-rounded (Baskerville) and heavy type faces (Scotch) permit a little more spacing between the words than do the lighter and more condensed type faces.

Colons, semicolons, quotation, exclamation and interrogation marks should be separated by an extra hair space from the words they adjoin; this also applies to the spacing between parentheses and the first and terminal letters enclosed when these letters are lower-case ascenders or descenders or capitals with upright stems, e.g. (liberated) not (liberated). Whether in text or display, spacing following a full point needs careful adjustment when the full point follows an abbreviated word or a sloping initial within a sentence, e.g.:

Charles A. Anderson

not   Charles A. Anderson

$2\frac{1}{4}$ in. $\times$ $5\frac{3}{8}$ in.

not $2\frac{1}{4}$ in. $\times$ $5\frac{3}{8}$ in.

Indention of paragraphs should be one em, but the first paragraph following a heading or subheading should be set full out. Copious extracts should be either indented or set a size or two smaller than the main type of the text (page 42).

There are often special reasons for supporting those who prefer to set copious quotations in smaller type. Poetry that is quoted might conceivably have many overrun lines if set in the same size type as the text; this would be easily avoided if set smaller. Again, many letters quoted in full to give the necessary background to some specific section would result in a book of unnecessary bulk if the letters were printed in the same type size as the text. On the other hand, in a case where the book consists of a collection of letters we might perhaps reverse the procedure and print the letters in the type size chosen for the main text with the editor's commentary set smaller.

Footnotes should be set in type two sizes smaller than the text. The exception to this is found when the printer is limited in his stock to so few sizes of any one type face as to make it impossible. In such cases the text and footnote, being of the same size or nearly so, might advantageously be separated by a thin short metal rule (about two ems long at most) placed to range at the left-hand edge of the type area.

In addition to footnotes, there will be some books with annotations which can only be printed through the use of 'cut-in' or 'hanging shoulder' notes. The former, as their name suggests, are notes printed in a small space cut into the text. The type in which these notes are set must necessarily be very small in size.

The space for hanging shoulder notes is strictly limited, for obvious reasons. The width of the type area available will inevitably be very narrow and lines will tend to be uneven in length. Uneven lines should range on the left for a right-hand page and on the right for a left-hand page on that side of the marginal note which adjoins the text. The first line of a marginal note should be aligned with the relevant lines of text whether the marginal note is set in the same size as the text type or smaller (page 51). When the note is unduly long, it might be necessary to run on part of it at the bottom of the text.

Pagination of the body of the book (exclusive of preliminaries) begins in arabic numerals on the first page of the main text or on the half-title to the text. It is customary for the pagination to be printed centred at the bottom of the text or set on the left and right extremes of the type area either at the bottom of the page or at the top ranged with the headline. When the pagination is at the top, the numerals are allowed for but not actually printed on the pages of the chapter openings. Similarly, page numbers are not necessarily printed on any full pages of illustrations in the text, particularly when the size of the blocks exceeds the size of the type area.

He never lived in Suffolk again. In 1813 his wife died; for seventeen years she had been ailing and almost out of her mind, yet Crabbe had never ceased to love and cherish her. Before he crossed England to take over a living in Wiltshire, he came back to Aldeburgh for a last visit to one of his sisters. On a lovely day in May he rode over to Parham and Glemham to wander among the fields and woods he loved so well, and to see once more the houses where he and Sarah had spent such happy years. He did not return till late at night, and in his pocket-book were found these lines:

> Yes, I behold again the place,
>   The seat of joy, the source of pain;
> It brings in view the form and face
>   That I must never see again.
>
> The night-bird's song that sweetly floats
>   On this soft gloom—this balmy air,
> Brings to the mind her sweeter notes
>   That I again must never hear.
>
> Lo! yonder shines that window's light,
>   My guide, my token, heretofore;
> And now again it shines as bright,
>   When those dear eyes can shine no more.
>
> Then hurry from this place away!
>   It gives not now the bliss it gave;
> For death has made its charm his prey,
>   And joy is buried in her grave.

With this, one of the best lyrics he ever wrote, I will leave the story of Crabbe, for it concerns Suffolk no more, although, no matter how far away

Quoted poem set a size smaller than author's prose. In this case it is not done to avoid broken lines but to give clearly to the reader, through surrounding white space, the shape of the poem and its difference in temper from the matter surrounding it.

address graceful. Her manners had all the elegance which her husband's wanted. But they would have been improved by some share of his frankness and warmth; and her visit was long enough to detract something from their first admiration, by showing that, though perfectly well bred, she was reserved, cold, and had nothing to say for herself beyond the most commonplace inquiry or remark.

Conversation, however, was not wanted, for Sir John was very chatty, and Lady Middleton had taken the wise precaution of bringing with her their eldest child, a fine little boy about six years old; by which means there was one subject always to be recurred to by the ladies in case of extremity, for they had to inquire his name and age, admire his beauty, and ask him questions which his mother answered for him, while he hung about her and held down his head, to the great surprise of her ladyship, who wondered at his being so shy before company, as he could make noise enough at home. On every formal visit a child ought to be of the party, by way of provision for discourse. In the present case it took up ten minutes to determine whether the boy were most like his father or mother, and in what particular he resembled either, for of course everybody differed, and everybody was astonished at the opinion of the others.

An opportunity was soon to be given to the Dashwoods of debating on the rest of the children, as Sir John would not leave the house without securing their promise of dining at the Park the next day.

CHAPTER VII

BARTON PARK was about half a mile from the cottage. The ladies had passed near it in their way along the valley, but it was screened from their view at home by the projection of a hill. The house was large and handsome; and the Middletons lived in a style of equal hospitality and elegance. The former was for Sir John's gratification, the latter for that of his lady. They were scarcely ever without some friends staying with them in the house, and they kept more company of every kind than any other family in the neighbourhood. It was necessary to the happiness of both; for however dissimilar in temper and outward behaviour, they strongly resembled each other in that total want

[27]

An occasion when a chapter opening is not given a new page.

HEAD-LINES

As already mentioned, the head-lines ('running heads') of a book are most generally in two parts, the title of the book on the left-hand page and the chapter title (often of necessity abbreviated) on the right.[1] The right-hand head-line is, on occasion, a heading, known as a topical head, epitomizing the main subject-matter of each page and would consequently be supplied by the author. The head-line serves several purposes, the most important being that it enables the reader to pick up a chapter or section of the book and speedily find a rough indication of what is in the page. The head-line in the less ephemeral kind of book is often invaluable when a book is physically disintegrating, for it then becomes a guide to future librarians and restorative bookbinders, particularly if the title or other vital pages of the book are missing. The head-line imparts typographical character to the page through the manner and choice of type employed.

Fiction presents a peculiar problem of its own with regard to head-lines; where they are repeated on both sides of the page, the effect is tedious. It will be readily understood, therefore, why fiction is often printed without head-lines. In certain books, when there are titles to chapters, it is not infrequent to have the title of the chapter as the left-hand head-line, and on the right-hand page a head-line summarizing the main subject-matter on that particular page.

The head-line is most conveniently set in the capitals, small capitals or italic of the type face and type size of the text page. Small capitals are preferable for most books, as not only do they strike the right degree of emphasis but they are space-saving in width compared with capitals. Capitals tend to produce over-emphasis and monotony but are nevertheless useful on a large page and when the words of the head-line are short. Capitals and small capitals should be letter-spaced to attain full legibility.

[1] Many typographers however believe that it is not necessary to keep reminding the reader of the title of his book and prefer to print the chapter title on both pages.—Ed.

Head-lines should be separated from the text by six points (two thick leads) white space or the equivalent depth of a line of the type in which the book is set.

The use of italic capitals for short head-lines presents many subtleties and difficulties, and we take this opportunity of examining italic capitals in general. Compared on the following pages, we have the words *TRANSVAAL LAWYER REPRIEVED* set in 12 pt. italic capitals in sixteen of the type faces shown on pages 14–17. These italic capitals are set both close and letterspaced. It is obvious immediately that the slope of the italic capitals is more even throughout in some type faces and irregular in others. If a book is set in Baskerville, Times, Imprint or other types with a fairly even slope to all the letters, it would be reasonable to set headlines in italic capitals if desired, but it would be inadvisable in Bell, Caslon, Garamond or Walbaum, and types with similar very irregular slope to the italic capitals, even when the capitals are letter-spaced; the sharp fall-away of the *A* and *W* presents an unharmonious effect disturbing to the eye of the most unsophisticated reader. Similarly, in addition, the *R* of Blado adjoins any succeeding letter very awkwardly owing to the wide sweep of its tail. These types, in fact, were never designed with the purpose in view of setting whole words in italic capitals.[1]

The Perpetua and Times italics are more closely related to their roman than any other types; their italics might be called a sloping roman. The Baskerville italic is mildly decorative by the nature of its seven dandified capital letters, the *J K N Q T Y* and *Z* which border on being swash letters, and it is curious that no alternative letters were designed by Baskerville.

Head-lines set in capitals and lower-case italic can look agreeable, while plain rules supporting the head-lines can, on occasion, add variety and richness to a page (see page 48).

---

[1] See 'Towards an Ideal Italic', by Stanley Morison. *The Fleuron,* No. V. 1926.

BASKERVILLE

TRANSVAAL LAWYER REPRIEVED

TRANSVAAL LAWYER REPRIEVED

BELL

TRANSVAAL LAWYER REPRIEVED

TRANSVAAL LAWYER REPRIEVED

BEMBO

TRANSVAAL LAWYER REPRIEVED

TRANSVAAL LAWYER REPRIEVED

BLADO

TRANSVAAL LAWYER REPRIEVED

TRANSVAAL LAWYER REPRIEVED

BODONI

TRANSVAAL LAWYER REPRIEVED

TRANSVAAL LAWYER REPRIEVED

CASLON

TRANSVAAL LAWYER REPRIEVED

TRANSVAAL LAWYER REPRIEVED

CENTAUR

TRANSVAAL LAWYER REPRIEVED

TRANSVAAL LAWYER REPRIEVED

EHRHARDT

TRANSVAAL LAWYER REPRIEVED

TRANSVAAL LAWYER REPRIEVED

Italic capitals closely set and letter-spaced.

46

SETTING OF THE TEXT

FOURNIER
TRANSVAAL LAWYER REPRIEVED
TRANSVAAL LAWYER REPRIEVED

GARAMOND
TRANSVAAL LAWYER REPRIEVED
TRANSVAAL LAWYER REPRIEVED

IMPRINT
TRANSVAAL LAWYER REPRIEVED
TRANSVAAL LAWYER REPRIEVED

PERPETUA
TRANSVAAL LAWYER REPRIEVED
TRANSVAAL LAWYER REPRIEVED

PLANTIN
TRANSVAAL LAWYER REPRIEVED
TRANSVAAL LAWYER REPRIEVED

SCOTCH
TRANSVAAL LAWYER REPRIEVED
TRANSVAAL LAWYER REPRIEVED

TIMES
TRANSVAAL LAWYER REPRIEVED
TRANSVAAL LAWYER REPRIEVED

WALBAUM
TRANSVAAL LAWYER REPRIEVED
TRANSVAAL LAWYER REPRIEVED

Italic capitals closely set and letter-spaced.

Date Gems

Beat $\frac{1}{3}$ cup butter and 1 cup castor sugar to a cream; add 2 eggs well beaten, $\frac{1}{2}$ cup milk, $1\frac{3}{4}$ cup flour, 2 teaspoons baking powder, $\frac{1}{2}$ teaspoon ground ginger, $\frac{1}{4}$ teaspoon grated nutmeg, $\frac{1}{4}$ teaspoon powdered cloves, and 1 cupful chopped dates. Mix well and divide into buttered and floured gem pans, and bake in a moderate oven for 25 minutes. Cool on a cake-rack, and when cold decorate each with icing sugar moistened with orange juice and a good squeeze of lemon, and top with a stoned date. (*Beryl Freeman's Recipe.*)—E. C. (2).

Date Moons

Put $\frac{1}{2}$ lb. dates, stoned, through the meat chopper, and add $\frac{1}{2}$ cup walnuts and 2 oz. candied ginger coarsely cut. Knead and roll into sausages, using powdered sugar to prevent sticking. Serve cut in thin slices. (*Moyna Macgill's Recipe.*)—E. C. (2).

DEWBERRY

The name given in the U.S.A. to any trailing *Blackberry* as opposed to the 'Bush' or upright *Blackberries*. There are different varieties of *Dewberries* which are cultivated as garden small fruit. The chief value of the *Dewberry* at the market gardener's point of view is that it ripens its fruit at least a week or two in advance of the *Blackberries*. It is used in cookery and confectionery in the same ways as *Blackberries* (q.v.).

DURIAN

The oval or globose fruit of the *Durio zibethinus*, a Malayan tree which is extensively grown in the East and Far East. The flavour of the *Durian*, when at the right degree of ripeness and just picked, is delicious; so is its soft, cream-coloured pulp; but its smell, which is strong at all times, very soon becomes foul when the fruit is over-ripe or kept for any time after being picked. The seeds can also be roasted and eaten like chestnuts.

D. Fairchild calls the *Durian* 'the most remarkable fruit in the world'. The fruits weigh from 5 to 10 lb. and are about the size of small coconuts and completely covered with sharp prickles.

FIG

The fruit of a number of different types of fig-trees. Figs may be divided into two main classes according to their shape, according to whether they are round, roundish or turbinate; or else long, pyriform or obovate. In each one of those two categories there are Figs with dark purple skin and others with green, or green tinged with brown. And in each case Figs may be further divided according to the colour of their pulp, which may be red or from white to opaline. The natural home of the *Fig* is the Mediterranean basin from Syria to the Canaries, but Smyrna Figs, which are the best, and *Caprifigs*, which are wild Figs, have been introduced in California, together with the insect that is responsible for their fertilization, and they are now well established there as well as in the Gulf States. In England, Figs ripen out of doors in some sheltered positions, but they are mostly grown under glass. In France, Spain, Portugal and Italy they are grown extensively.

Wherever Figs ripen out of doors they are eaten when freshly picked as one of the most delicious of dessert fruits, but they are mostly used commercially in the dried form, when they travel and keep well.

Fig Mould

Chop up 1 lb. of dried Figs and put them in a saucepan with 6 oz. of

Page showing head-line enlivened by a rule. The danger of this is that bad folding or cutting is shown up immediately by the rule.

THE CHAPTER OPENING

The chapter heading most commonly consists of the number of the chapter followed by the title. The chapter number may either consist of a plain (II, 2, 2) numeral or it may be preceded by the word CHAPTER. When there is a chapter title as well, this title takes first place in the reader's interest and should be set more prominently than the chapter number (or the head-line), e.g.:

CHAPTER I

THE VOLUNTARY EXILE

Both the chapter number and title are displayed lines and do not, therefore, require punctuation.

If the word CHAPTER is set in capitals, roman numerals should be used, unless the fount possesses modern numerals which range with the capitals, e.g.:

CHAPTER II (Walbaum with roman numeral)

CHAPTER 2 (Times with modern numeral)

not   CHAPTER 2 (Walbaum with old style numeral)

It will readily be seen that an old style numeral in juxta-position with capitals presents an awkward appearance.

A book is divided into chapters partly to provide a series of breaks which assist the reader by giving him a convenient amount of reading at a stretch, which he can adapt to his powers of con-centration and the amount of time at his disposal. Each chapter should, therefore, begin on a fresh page (left or right) and, to make this beginning doubly clear, it is a useful convention which causes a new chapter opening to be dropped a few lines down the page. An exception may be made in pocket editions and when condensation is imperative, in which case the chapter heading can run on without starting a new page (see page 43). The first word of the text of a new chapter requires special typographical treatment. The first word, which should not be indented, can most commonly be set either in:

(*a*) Capitals

(*b*) Small Capitals

(*c*) Capitals and Small Capitals.

(*a*) Capitals are satisfactory in a type where the capitals range lower than the ascenders, as in Bembo and Perpetua, but, in most other types, the use of capitals for the opening word of a chapter tends to over-emphasis. Some typographers consider however that the singling out of the first word gives an emphasis which may be invidious. This applies also to the word which follows a dropped initial (see page 52).

(*b*) Conversely, small capitals tend towards understatement unless used in conjunction with an initial letter.

(*c*) Capitals and small capitals strike a good medium and are, perhaps, the most convenient for the first word of the chapter opening in the average book. Whichever of the above alternatives is adopted, the capitals and small capitals should be letter-spaced.

> SOME people have a foolish way of not minding, or pretending not to mind, what they eat. For my part, I mind my belly very studiously, and very carefully; for I look upon it, that he who does not mind his belly will hardly mind anything else.
>
> (*a*) 10 on 11 pt. Bembo, opening in capitals.

> DEPEND upon it that if a man talks of his misfortunes there is something in them that is not disagreeable to him, for where there is nothing but pure misery, there never is any recourse to the mention of it.
>
> (*b*) 10 on 11 pt. Plantin, opening in small capitals.

> EVERY man who comes into the world has need of friends. If he has to get them for himself, half his life is spent before his merit is known. Relations are a man's ready friends who support him. When a man is in real distress, he flies into the arms of his relations.
>
> (*c*) 10 on 11 pt. Ehrhardt, opening in capitals and small capitals.

PART II

Section 3

In Tabula Smaragdina.

forged out, we need not examine the sparks which irregularly fly from it.

LET well-weighed Considerations, not stiff and peremptory Assumptions, guide thy discourses, Pen and Actions. To begin or continue our works like Trismegistus of old, *Verum, certè verum, atque verissimum est*, would sound arrogantly unto present Ears in this strict enquiring Age, wherein, for the most part, *Probably,* and *Perhaps,* will hardly serve to mollify the Spirit of captious Contradictors. If Cardan saith that a Parrot is a beautiful Bird, Scaliger will set his Wits o' work to prove it a deformed Animal. The Compage of all Physical Truths is not so closely jointed, but opposition may find intrusion, nor always so closely maintained, as not to suffer attrition. Many Positions seem quodlibetically constituted, and like a Delphian Blade will cut on both sides. Some Truths seem almost Falshoods, and some Falshoods almost Truths; wherein Falshood and Truth seem almost equilibriously stated, and but a few grains of distinction to bear down the ballance. Some have digged deep, yet glanced by the Royal Vein; and a Man may come unto the *Pericardium,* but not the Heart of Truth. Besides, many things are known, as some are seen, that is by Parallaxis, or at some distance from their true and proper beings, the superficial regard of things having a different aspect from their true and central Natures. And this moves sober Pens unto suspensory and timorous assertions, nor presently to obtrude them as Sibyl's leaves, which after considerations may find to be but folious apparences, and not the central and vital interiours of Truth.

Section 4

VALUE the judicious, and let not mere acquests in minor parts of Learning gain thy preexistimation. 'Tis an unjust way of compute to magnify a weak Head for some Latin abilities, and to undervalue a solid Judgment, because he knows not the genealogy of Hector. When

[122]

PART II

Lewis the Eleventh. *Qui nescit dissimulare nescit Regnare.*

that notable King of France* would have his Son to know but one sentence in Latin, had it been a good one, perhaps it had been enough. Natural parts and good Judgments rule the World. States are not governed by Ergotisms. Many have Ruled well who could not perhaps define a Commonwealth, and they who understand not the Globe of the Earth command a great part of it. Where natural Logick prevails not, artificial too often faileth. Where Nature fills the Sails, the Vessel goes smoothly on, and when Judgment is the Pilot, the Ensurance need not be high. When Industry builds upon Nature, we may expect Pyramids: where that foundation is wanting, the structure must be low. They do most by Books, who could do much without them, and he that chiefly ows himself unto himself is the substantial Man.

Section 5

LET thy Studies be free as thy Thoughts and Contemplations, but fly not only upon the wings of Imagination; joyn Sense unto Reason, and Experiment unto Speculation, and so give life unto Embryon Truths, and Verities yet in their Chaos. There is nothing more acceptable unto the Ingenious World, than this noble Eluctation of Truth; wherein, against the tenacity of Prejudice and Prescription, this Century now prevaileth. What Libraries of new Volumes aftertimes will behold, and in what a new World of Knowledge the eyes of our Posterity may be happy, a few Ages may joyfully declare; and is but a cold thought unto those who cannot hope to behold this Exantlation of Truth, or that obscured Virgin half out of the Pit. Which might make some content with a commutation of the time of their lives, and to commend the Fancy of the Pythagorean metempsychosis; whereby they might hope to enjoy this happiness in their third or fourth selves, and behold that in Pythagoras, which they now but foresee in Euphorbus*. The World, which took but six days to make, is like to take six thousand to make out: mean

Ipse ego, nam memini, Trojani in tempore belli Panthoides Euphorbus eram. [Ovid, Metam. xv. 160.]

[123]

Page opening showing hanging shoulder notes with the uneven lines ranged inwards (line-block reduced).

Where the first word of a chapter is a single letter, i.e. A or I, it is desirable to include in the display the word following in order to balance the initial.

Initial letters emphasize a chapter opening to a marked degree. They can be either raised or dropped. The most simple raised initial is a capital letter of the text type set two sizes larger, but some printers have types that impart a more decorative effect. All dropped initial letters must appear to range with the lines of the matter which adjoins, and spacing to the right must be regulated according to the shape of the letter. The remaining letters of the word will generally be set in capitals or small capitals to support the initial whether it is raised or dropped. In all cases initials must fit snugly (page 53 (*a*) and (*b*)). Dropped initials need to be of a certain size to achieve an agreeable effect, therefore when they are used with 11 pt. type or under, it would be unwise to use them smaller than three-line. The capitals of a good type with the beard filed off make adequate initial letters if the printer has no initial letters in his stock (page 54).

An initial letter is, on occasion, used for the opening chapter of the book only. Certainly the opening of the main text of a book is made unmistakably clear by such emphasis. But this emphasis can also be achieved either by printing the title or an abbreviated title of the book at the top of the opening page, above the chapter number, or by introducing a second half-title page[1] on the last right-hand page preceding the opening of the main text.

In any case care must be exercised to ensure that an initial letter does not strike a discordant note on the opening page of the text when the title of the book is also displayed in the upper portion of the page. If the display is simply set in the text type, an initial, even a highly decorative initial, can generally be safely used (page 55). On the other hand if the title is set in a decorative or semi-decorative type, or in some special manner, it would be well not to use a dropped initial letter at all.

[1] This is an American practice, only rarely followed in English typography. —Ed.

THE Revelation of Jesus Christ, which God gave unto him, to shew unto his servants things which must shortly come to pass; and 'he sent and signified it by his angel unto his servant John : ⁋ 2 Who bare record of the word of God, and of the testimony of Jesus Christ,

(*a*) Five-line initial. The serif of the left arm of the T overlaps the type measure, resulting in the initial being placed correctly *optically*.

ALMIGHTY GOD, our heavenly Father, who of his great mercy hath promised forgiveness of sins to all them that with hearty repentance

(*b*) Three-line initial with the serif of the left tail of the A overlapping the type measure, resulting in the initial being placed correctly *optically*. The remainder of the word in capitals is drawn in towards the initial, as always in the case of a dropped initial A.

WE do not presume to come to this thy Table, O merciful Lord, trusting in our own righteousness, but in thy manifold and great mercies. We are not worthy so much as to gather up the crumbs under thy

(*c*) Ill-fitting initial. The initial falls below the third line and is consequently neither a three- nor a four-line initial. The left-hand serif does not overlap the type measure.

A B C D E F G

Caslon Titling

H I J K L M N

Lyons Capitals

N O P Q R S

Bembo Titling

H I J L M N O

Old Face Open Titling

A B C D E F

Perpetua Titling

A S T U V W

Centaur Titling

Examples of types suitable for initials: titling, which has no
beard at the foot, or capitals with the beard removed.

J. van Krimpen

S. H. de Roos

Anna Simons

Eric Gill

Percy Smith

F. W. Kleukens

A selection of plain and decorative initial letters.

55

A B C D E G

Gill Floriated

A Victorian revival

CDEFG

Fry's Baskerville

Scroll Shaded

A selection of plain and decorative initial letters.

CHAPTER XXV

Doubts—Wise King of Jerusalem—Let Me See—A Thousand Years—Nothing New—The Crowd—The Hymn—Faith—Charles Wesley—There He Stood—Farewell, Brother—Death—Sun, Moon, and Stars—Wind on the Heath.

THERE was one question which I was continually asking myself at this period, and which has more than once met the eyes of the reader who has followed me through the last chapter. 'What is truth?' I had involved myself imperceptibly in a dreary labyrinth of doubt, and, whichever way I turned, no reasonable prospect of extricating myself appeared. The means by which I had brought myself into this situation may be briefly told: I had inquired into many matters, in order that I might become wise, and I had read and pondered over the words of the wise, so called, till I had made myself master of the sum of human wisdom —namely, that everything is enigmatical, and that man is an enigma to himself; thence the cry of 'What is truth?' I had ceased to believe in the truth of that in which I had hitherto trusted, and yet could find nothing in which I could put any fixed or deliberate belief. I was, indeed, in a labyrinth! In what did I not doubt! With respect to crime and virtue I was in doubt: I doubted that the one was blameable and the other praiseworthy. Are not all things subjected to the law of necessity? Assuredly; time and chance govern all things: yet how can this be? alas!

Then there was myself; for what was I born? Are not all things born to be forgotten? That's incomprehensible; yet is it not so? Those butterflies fall and

Chapter opening from *Lavengro,* with synopsis of contents and a raised initial supported by small capitals.

57

CORNELII TACITI
DE ORIGINE, SITU, MORIBUS AC POPULIS
GERMANORUM

GERMANIA omnis a Gallis Raetisque et Pannoniis Rheno et Danuvio fluminibus, a Sarmatis Dacisque mutuo metu aut montibus seperatur: cetera Oceanus ambit, latos sinus et insularum immensa spatia complectens, nuper cognitis quibusdam gentibus ac regibus, quos bellum aperuit. Rhenus, Raeticarum Alpium inaccesso ac praecipiti vertice ortus, modico flexu in occidentem versus septentrionali Oceano miscetur. Danuvius, molli et clementer edito montis Abnobae iugo effusus, pluris populos adit, donec in Ponticum mare sex meatibus erumpat: septimum os paludibus hauritur.

IPSOS Germanos indigenas crediderim minimeque aliarum gentium adventibus et hospitiis mixtos, quia nec terra olim sed classibus advehebantur qui mutare sedes quaerebant et immensus ultra utque sic dixerim adversus Oceanus raris ab orbe nostro navibus aditur. Quis porro, praeter periculum horridi et ignoti maris, Asia aut Africa aut Italia relicta Germaniam peteret, informen terris, asperam caelo, tristem cultu aspectuque, nisi si patria sit? Celebrant carminibus antiquis, quod unum apud illos memoriae et annalium genus est, Tuistonem, deum terra editum, et filium Mannum originem gentis conditoresque. Manno tris filios assignant, e quorum nominibus proximi Oceano Ingaevones, medii Herminones, ceteri Istaevones vocentur. Quidam, ut in licentia vetustatis, pluris deo ortos plurisque gentis appellationes, Marsos Gambrivios Suebos Vandilios, affirmant, eaque vera et antiqua nomina. Ceterum Germaniae vocabulum recens et nuper additum, quoniam qui primi Rhenum transgressi Gallos expulerint ac nunc Tungri, tunc Germani vocati sint. Ita nationis nomen, non gentis, evaluisse paulatim, ut omnes primum a victore ob metum, mox etiam a se ipsis invento nomine Germani vocarentur.

FUISSE apud eos et Herculem memorant, primumque omnium virorum fortium ituri in proelia canunt. Sunt illis haec quoque carmina quorum relatu, quem barditum vocant, accendunt animos futuraeque pugnae fortunam ipso cantu augurantur. Terrent enim trepidantve prout sonuit acies, nec tam vocis ille quam virtutis concentus videtur. Affectatur praecipue asperitas soni et fractum murmur, obiectis ad os scutis, quo plenior et gravior vox repercussu intumescat. Ceterum et Vlixen quidam opinantur longo illo et

Page with decorative initials and plain setting of title.

(Line-block reduced)

THE PRINTING OF PLAYS

The setting of a play has its own typographical necessities. Whilst the choice of type and the margins of the page are subject to the same principles as the printing of prose, it is of primary importance to be able to pick out the part of each character with speed, and the stage directions should be clearly differentiated from the rest of the text. The names of the different characters can be set either in capitals and lower-case italic, capitals and small capitals, or in even small capitals at the beginning of the line, but in each case the text following should be indented. This indention of the part throws the player's name into strong relief. The stage directions should be in italic. Square brackets are used to enclose stage directions when these appear within the dialogue (page 61). The head-line should include the number of the act and the scene number, when there is more than one scene in the act. When a play is printed for reading rather than for use by actors, the names of the characters may be centred above the part to be spoken (page 62). This method will undoubtedly result in a handsome page for leisurely reading, but it results, too, in a longer book. In this case the names of characters should be set in capitals or small capitals to ensure that there will be no possibility of confusion with any directions set in italic.

It is rarely necessary for a play to be printed with a table of contents. Instead it is usual to print a *Dramatis Personae* which consists of a list of the characters with the addition, when relevant, of their ranks, professions, etc., and their relation to each other, viz:

BASILIO, *King of Poland*
SEGISMUNDO, *Basilio's son*
ASTOLFO, *Duke of Muscovy*
CLOTALDO, *Segismundo's keeper*
CLARIN, *Servant to Rosaura*
ESTRELLA, *Basilio's niece*
ROSAURA, *A lady of Muscovy*

GENTLEMEN, SOLDIERS, ETC.

AMIENS: And I'll sing it.

JAQUES: Thus it goes.

> *If it do come to pass, that any man turn ass:*
> *Leaving his wealth and ease,*
> *A stubborn will to please,*
> *Ducdame, ducdame, ducdame:*
> *Here shall he see, gross fools as he,*
> *And if he will come to me.*

AMIENS: What's that ducdame?

JAQUES: 'Tis a Greek invocation, to call fools into a circle. I'll go sleep if I can: if I cannot, I'll rail against all the first-born in Egypt.

AMIENS: And I'll go see the Duke, his banquet is prepar'd.

Exeunt

II. 6

Enter Orlando and Adam

ADAM: Dear master, I can go no further: O I die for food. Here lie I down, and measure out my grave. Farewell kind master.

ORLANDO: Why how now Adam? No greater heart in thee: live a little, comfort a little, cheer thyself a little. If this uncouth Forest yield any thing savage, I will either be food for it, or bring it for food to thee: thy conceit is nearer death, than thy powers. For my sake be comfortable, hold death awhile at the arm's end: I will here be with thee presently, and if I bring thee not something to eat, I will give thee leave to die: but if thou diest before I come, thou art a mocker of my labour. Well said, thou look'st cheerly, and I'll be with thee quickly: yet thou liest in the bleak air. Come, I will bear thee to some shelter, and thou shalt not die for lack of a dinner,

45

Page from play in prose and verse. Head-line displays both act and scene number. Bold type is used for commencement of new scene (arabic numeral), with the number of the act repeated (roman numeral).

VOYNITSKY [*to* SONYA, *passing his hand over her hair*]. My child, how my heart aches! Oh, if only you knew how my heart aches!

SONYA. There is nothing for it. We must go on living! [*a pause*]. We shall go on living, Uncle Vanya! We shall live through a long, long chain of days and weary evenings; we shall patiently bear the trials which fate sends us; we shall work for others, both now and in our old age, and have no rest; and when our time comes we shall die without a murmur, and there beyond the grave we shall say that we have suffered, that we have wept, that life has been bitter to us, and God will have pity on us, and you and I, uncle, dear uncle, shall see a light that is bright, lovely, beautiful. We shall rejoice and look back at these troubles of ours with tenderness, with a smile—and we shall rest. I have faith, uncle; I have fervent, passionate faith. [*Slips on her knees before him and lays her head on his hands; in a weary voice.*] We shall rest!

TELYEGIN *softly plays on the guitar.*

SONYA. We shall rest! We shall hear the angels; we shall see all Heaven lit with radiance; we shall see all earthly evil, all our sufferings, drowned in mercy which will fill the whole world, and our life will be peaceful, gentle and sweet as a caress. I have faith, I have faith [*wipes away his tears with her handkerchief*]. Poor Uncle Vanya, you are crying. [*Through her tears.*] You have had no joy in your life, but wait, Uncle Vanya, wait. We shall rest [*puts her arms round him*]. We shall rest! [*The watchman taps.*]

TELYEGIN *plays softly;* MARYA VASSILYEVNA *makes notes on the margin of her pamphlet;* MARINA *knits her stocking.*

SONYA. We shall rest!

CURTAIN DROPS SLOWLY

Setting of play in prose. Square brackets used only when directions appear within the dialogue. Text indented so that each character speaking can be quickly picked out.

LEONIDAS

Did you not merit, as you do, my heart,
Love gives esteem, and then it gives desert.
But if I basely could forget my vow,
Poor helpless innocence, what would you do?

PALMYRA

In woods, and plains, where first my love began,
There would I live, retired from faithless man:
I'd sit all day within some lonely shade,
Or that close arbour which your hands have made:
I'd search the groves, and every tree, to find
Where you had carved our names upon the rind:
Your hook, your scrip, all that was yours I'd keep,
And lay them by me when I went to sleep.
Thus would I live: And maidens, when I die,
Upon my hearse white true-love knots should tie;
And thus my tomb should be inscribed above,
Here the forsaken Virgin rests from love.

LEONIDAS

Think not that time or fate shall e'er divide
Those hearts, which love and mutual vows have tied.
But we must part; farewell, my love.

PALMYRA

Till when?

LEONIDAS

Till the next age of hours we meet again.
Meantime, we may,
When near each other we in public stand,
Contrive to catch a look, or steal a hand:
Fancy will every touch and glance improve;
And draw the most spirituous parts of love.
Our souls sit close, and silently within,
And their own web from their own entrails spin;
And when eyes meet far off, our sense is such,
That, spider-like, we feel the tenderest touch.
                                        [*Exeunt.*

Page from a play in couplets, with characters centred.

THE PRINTING OF POETRY

The printing of poetry is more complex than the printing of prose and any rules must allow for many exceptions. Poetry is more slowly and deliberately read than prose, which means that the reader is more than usually aware of typographical qualities. The choice of a good type face and its point size is governed by the importance of avoiding broken lines, therefore the types with a narrow set, and in relatively small sizes, are the most suitable, such as Bembo, Caslon, Ehrhardt, Fournier, Times and Walbaum. Type that is too large is a disadvantage because it means that the shape of the poem may be lost, and the shape of a poem is not only pleasing to the eye, but is a help to the mind in grasping the rhythmic character of the poem. This is important in much con- temporary poetry when no traditional metrical scheme is followed. Even when using types small in point size and narrow in set, it is sometimes necessary to exceed the type measure for an occasional line to avoid a break. In the setting of poetry all types should

(*a*)   W HAT dire Offence from am'rous Causes springs,
        What mighty contests rise from trivial Things,
        I sing—This verse to C ARYL, Muse! is due;
        This, ev'n *Belinda* may vouchsafe to view;
        Slight is the Subject, but not so the Praise,
        If She inspire, and He approve, my Lays.

(*b*) W HAT dire Offence from am'rous Causes springs,
        What mighty contests rise from trivial Things,
        I sing—This verse to C ARYL, Muse! is due;
        This, ev'n *Belinda* may vouchsafe to view;
        Slight is the Subject, but not so the Praise,
        If She inspire, and He approve, my Lays.

(*a*) Set in 11 on 14 pt. Bembo, close set, middle space between the words.
(*b*) Set in 11 on 14 pt. Baskerville, wide set, thick space between the words.

be leaded and spacing between the words should be even; a middle space between each word. If the setting is amply leaded the space between the words may be increased (page 63), particularly when the type is wide on the body. Short-line poems should be indented to balance the margins, and the title of each poem should be centred on the *optical* centre of the poem, not on the first line, two very important points and a test of skill to the compositor. The shape of stanza forms should always be apparent on the page; where possible, in case of lyric poetry, the whole poem should be on a single page, but if this is impossible the break must be made between stanzas and not in the middle of a stanza. The space between stanzas depends, to a certain extent, on the amount of room to spare when the page is made up.

It is generally impracticable to incorporate running head-lines except where the book consists of one or two long poems. Where the book is an anthology, the reader likes to be able to pick out easily the contribution of each poet. Each author's name can be set as a shoulder note in the outer margins which would fulfil, in effect, a similar purpose to a head-line. The disadvantages are that shoulder notes take more time to compose and arrange and the margins must be on the generous side.

Folios are best at the bottom, either to the left or right of the page or centred. In cases where the poems themselves are numbered and where the folios are centred, the folios might well be enclosed in brackets.

The beginning of each poem is the equivalent of a new chapter opening in prose, and may have similar ceremonial treatment, such as raised or dropped initial letters or the first word of each poem set in capitals and small capitals. A dropped initial letter is most conveniently used when poems are set full out, as in the case of blank verse, heroic couplets and the Shakespearian sonnet: on the other hand a dropped initial letter tends to be disturbing if used with poems which include indented lines at their beginnings, or if the verse is short.

The printer should follow the poet's MS. for capitalization. If capitals are not used to begin every fresh line then they should only be used where indicated by the poet, either for emphasis or for punctuation (i.e. sense). When no punctuation is used and capitals are only used to indicate the beginning of a new sentence, it would avoid possible confusion if initial capitals were *not* used invariably at the beginning of each line.

Each line is set full out in heroic couplets, half-rhymes, the Shakespearian sonnet (see below) and blank verse. Quatrains of alternately four and three stress lines should not be set full out, nor should short lines in other stanza forms be set full out *where the shape of the stanza is important*.[1] Indention does not depend so much on rhyme but on length of line and consequent appearance of the poem. Short lines appearing in poems that are in the main decasyllabic are consequently indented.

LIKE as the waves make towards the pebbled shore,
So do our minutes hasten to their end;
Each changing place with that which goes before,
In secret toil all forwards do contend.
Nativity, once in the main of light,
Crawls to maturity, wherewith being crown'd,
Crooked eclipses 'gainst his glory fight,
And Time that gave doth now his gift confound.
Time doth transfix the flourish set on youth
And delves the parallels in beauty's brow,
Feeds on the rarities of nature's truth,
And nothing stands but for his scythe to mow:
 And yet to times in hope my verse shall stand,
 Praising thy worth, despite his cruel hand.

Shakespearian sonnet with a dropped initial
and last two rhymed lines indented.

[1]'For the very look of verse on the printed page excites definite expectations in the mind of the reader, just as a glimpse at a bill of fare excites certain digestive juices in one's body.' From *The Printing of Poetry*, by Walter de la Mare.

MUTABILITY

FROM low to high doth dissolution climb,
And sink from high to low, along a scale
Of awful notes, whose concord shall not fail;
A musical but melancholy chime,
Which they can hear who meddle not with crime,
Nor avarice, nor over-anxious care.
Truth fails not; but her outward forms that bear
The longest date do melt like frosty rime,
That in the morning whiten'd hill and plain
And is no more; drop like the tower sublime
Of yesterday, which royally did wear
His crown of weeds, but could not even sustain
Some casual shout that broke the silent air,
Or the unimaginable touch of Time.

Sonnet by Wordsworth, set in the same manner as the Shakespearian
sonnet, but without indented couplet at the end.

ON FIRST LOOKING INTO
CHAPMAN'S HOMER

MUCH have I travell'd in the realms of gold,
  And many goodly states and kingdoms seen;
  Round many western islands have I been
Which bards in fealty to Apollo hold.
Oft of one wide expanse had I been told
  That deep-brow'd Homer ruled as his demesne:
  Yet did I never breathe its pure serene
Till I heard Chapman speak out loud and bold:
Then felt I like some watcher of the skies
  When a new planet swims into his ken;
Or like stout Cortez, when with eagle eyes
  He stared at the Pacific—and all his men
Look'd at each other with a wild surmise—
  Silent, upon a peak in Darien.

Sonnet by Keats with variation of sequence of rhymes on the same sound.
Lines 1, 4, 5 and 8 rhyme on the same sound, lines 2, 3, 6 and 7 on another and are
set indented. There is no rhymed couplet at the end.

WE'LL GO NO MORE A-ROVING

So, we'll go no more a-roving
  So late into the night,
Though the heart be still as loving,
  And the moon be still as bright.

For the sword outwears its sheath,
  And the soul wears out the breast,
And the heart must pause to breathe.
  And love itself have rest.

Though the night was made for loving,
  And the day returns too soon,
Yet we'll go no more a-roving
  By the light of the moon.

Ballad by Byron, alternate rhymed lines indented.

WHEN LILACS LAST IN THE DOORYARD BLOOM'D

I

WHEN lilacs last in the dooryard bloom'd,
And the great star early droop'd in the western sky in the night,
I mourn'd, and yet shall mourn with ever-returning spring.

Ever-returning spring, trinity sure to me you bring,
Lilac blooming perennial and drooping star in the west,
And thought of him I love.

2

O powerful western fallen star!
O shades of night—O moody, tearful night!
O great star disappear'd—O the black murk that hides the star!
O cruel hands that hold me powerless—O helpless soul of me!
O harsh surrounding cloud that will not free my soul.

3

In the dooryard fronting an old farm-house near the white-wash'd palings,
Stands the lilac bush tall-growing with heart-shaped leaves of rich green,
With many a pointed blossom rising delicate, with the perfume strong I love,
With every leaf a miracle—and from this bush in the dooryard,
With delicate-color'd blossoms and heart-shaped leaves of rich green,
A sprig with its flower I break.

A setting of free verse from a poem by Walt Whitman.

67

REMEMBRANCE

Cold in the earth—and the deep snow piled above thee,
    Far, far removed, cold in the dreary grave!
Have I forgot, my only Love, to love thee,
    Sever'd at last by Time's all-severing wave?

Now, when alone, do my thoughts no longer hover
    Over the mountains, on that northern shore,
Resting their wings where heath and fern-leaves cover
    Thy noble heart for ever, ever more?

Cold in the earth—and fifteen wild Decembers
    From those brown hills have melted into spring:
Faithful, indeed, is the spirit that remembers
    After such years of change and suffering!

*Lyrical verse by Emily Brontë in a simple metrical scheme
with alternate rhymed lines indented.*

THE PRISONER

Still let my tyrants know, I am not doom'd to wear
Year after year in gloom and desolate despair;
A messenger of Hope comes every night to me,
And offers for short life, eternal liberty.

He comes with Western winds, with evening's wandering airs,
With that clear dusk of heaven that brings the thickest stars:
Winds take a pensive tone, and stars a tender fire,
And visions rise, and change, that kill me with desire.

Desire for nothing known in my maturer years,
When Joy grew mad with awe, at counting future tears:
When, if my spirit's sky was full of flashes warm,
I knew not whence they came, from sun or thunder-storm.

*Lyrical verse by Emily Brontë in a simple metrical scheme
with lines rhyming in couples, all set full out.*

THE MESSAGE

SEND home my long strayed eyes to me,
Which (oh) too long have dwelt on thee;
Yet since there they have learn'd such ill,
Such forc'd fashions,
And false passions,
That they be
Made by thee
Fit for no good sight, keep them still.

(a) Short lines centred optically on long lines (Donne).

EASTER WINGS

LORD, who createdst man in wealth and store,
Though foolishly he lost the same,
Decaying more and more,
Till he became
Most poore:
With thee
O let me rise
As larks, harmoniously,
And sing this day thy victories:
Then shall the fall further the flight in me.

(b) Poem set to harmonize typographically with the poet's intentions in relating shape and effect when reading (Herbert).

THE WOMAN I MET

A STRANGER, I threaded sunken-hearted
A lamp-lit crowd;
And anon there passed me a soul departed,
Who mutely bowed.
In my far-off youthful years I had met her,
Full-pulsed; but now, no more life's debtor,
Onward she slid
In a shroud that furs half-hid.

(c) Irregular setting with the same intention as above (Hardy).

Examples of irregularly set verses.

5

THE PRELIMINARY PAGES

THE preliminary pages, technically known as 'Prelims', are a very important section of a book and include all the introductory pages preceding the main text. Prelims are sometimes few, consisting of, perhaps, a half-title, title, imprint, and contents pages, or they may comprise considerably more items occupying many pages, made up of half-title, title, history of the book and printer' imprint, dedication, acknowledgements, contents, list of illustrations, preface, introduction and corrigenda or errata. (For order of Prelims see page 8.)

The Prelims are set and made up after the galley proofs of the text have been put into final form in page proof, and it has consequently been ascertained that there are no further corrections or additions to be made nor any alterations in the pagination. Text pages are paginated in ordinary figures (arabic) 1, 2, 3, etc., whilst roman lower-case numerals are used for the pagination of the Prelims, i, ii, iii, iv, etc.[1]

This separation in the manner of the pagination is most useful. The Introduction, for instance, is usually written when the book is in its final page form, so that the page references and quotations taken from the text by the writer of the Introduction to clarify his meaning can be verified. Likewise, the Contents page and List of Illustrations can only be completed when the pagination of the text is complete. The Corrigenda is the final operation for it makes its regrettable but sometimes necessary appearance after the body of the book has been printed.

The division of the pagination serves other useful purposes. The body of the book can go to press whilst the Prelims are being compiled, set and proofed. The Prelims themselves can be subject to alteration or addition until they go to press without risking the expense and entailing the inconvenience of repaginating the whole book.

[1] But see page 8.

THE HALF-TITLE

From the point of view of the reader, the title-page is the first page of interest in a book, and, at a first glance, the half-title might appear to be superfluous. But the half-title fulfils useful purposes. It must be printed with the Prelims and this ensures that the paper of the page facing the title-page is of the same kind as the rest of the book and not a page of the endpapers. The half-title page also protects the title-page from any glue or its chemical constituents which may percolate through from the binding boards, and it helps, in general, to protect the title-page during the various stages of binding. The half-title plays a modest and strictly utilitarian part, and needs very simple typographic display. Usually the title of the book only is set in capitals in the same size of the type used in the text, set centred or slightly to the left, well above the optical centre of the page. If it is desired to print a list of works previously published by an author, this can conveniently be printed on the verso of the half-title, neatly displayed in small type.

THE TITLE-PAGE

The title-page has been a prominent typographic feature of the book ever since printing emerged from the *incunabula* period. It not only lends itself to skill and variety of typographical treatment but reflects the typographic quality of the whole book, and it is no accident that a third of the five hundred or so plates of Mr. Stanley Morison's monumental *Four Centuries of Fine Printing* should display title-pages. Moreover the same author has stated in his *First Principles of Typography* that 'The history of printing is in a large measure the history of the title-page'.

During the present century title-pages have become noticeably simpler both in their display and in the economy of words used. Striking and decorative emphasis appears now to centre on the book-jacket, which has attained a far greater importance than ever before as a means of advertisement and as an immediate attraction to the bookseller and book buyer. But the book-jacket is a transitory thing, liable to become quickly soiled, torn or removed and, therefore, serves only to give a pleasing first impression. Simple or elaborate, the title-page holds an assured place for the serious buyer, both for the information it gives and for the permanent degree to which it attracts the owner and reader of the book by its typographic style, with or without graphic ornamentation.

The title-page most commonly displays, in the following order, the title of the book, the name of the author, the publisher's imprint with place and date of publication.[1]

This is usually the minimum amount of information that must be given, but often a title-page must show considerably more, including a subtitle, editor, translator, illustrator, number of plates, number of volumes and a quotation. Where a book extends into separate volumes, the complete number of volumes should be stated if this is known in advance as well as the actual volume number of each book.

THE DISPLAY

The title and subtitle of a book are the most emphasized feature of a title-page display, followed by the name of the author and gradually diminishing in emphasis down to the address of the publisher and the place and date of publication, set in graduated sizes of type according to the relative importance of the items to be displayed. There are some exceptions. For instance, in the case of a particular translation from a Latin or Greek classic, as the *Iliad* of Homer, translated by Alexander Pope, the name of the translator should have the typographical prominence usually given to the author.

But in general, the title, subtitle and name of the author should be set in capitals or small capitals. Small capitals, and lower case

[1] Some publishers prefer the date of publication to be on the verso of the title-page. The reason for this appears to be that where a new book has remained in the bookshop unsold for some time, this distressing fact might escape immediate notice.—Ed.

with roman and italic, are at the printer's disposal for display of subsidiary matter, in addition to capitals in small sizes.

The main word of the title should not be broken, although the article attached to the word chosen for the largest size of display may be set in a separate line in the same sized type or smaller, and there are other occasions when this can be done (page 85).

It is on the whole an admirable tradition that the main headings of the title-page are set in sizes larger than the size of the capital of the text; it lends unmistakable clarity to the page, and taken in conjunction with the subsidiary matter (some of which might be smaller in size than the text) it enables the title-page to have an harmonious link with the text pages. Care should be taken not to set the main display in too large a size, and here perhaps there is a partial check owing to the desirability of avoiding broken words. No other word or line in a book should be set larger than the largest size of type on the title-page.

The basic arrangement of a title-page is conditioned by the wording, and by this we mean the number of words and their length, together with the number of items to be displayed. It is as well, therefore, to have no preconceived ideas of a style, and attempts should be resisted to force squared (broad), asymmetrical or tapered (triangular) effects. Where there is very little wording to be set, the title-page (if unornamented and set in reasonable display sizes) will contain a large amount of white space between the upper part—title and author, and the lower part—publisher and place. This is quite natural and within its limits can be treated through the right juxtaposition of type sizes, coupled with meticulous spacing of letters and lines displayed in the right position on the page (page 74).

The graduated sizes of the types used, coupled with the clarity of a title-page setting as a whole, make it unnecessary to have full points at the end of display lines. These would serve no useful purpose, while their inclusion would throw out of harmony the visual balance of the lines.

GEORGE BORROW
LAVENGRO

THE SCHOLAR · THE GIPSY · THE PRIEST

With an Introduction

by

HUGH WALPOLE

Illustrated with sixteen lithographs in colour
and pen drawings

by

BARNETT FREEDMAN

VOLUME I

Printed for the members of
THE LIMITED EDITIONS CLUB
AT THE CURWEN PRESS
LONDON
1936

Title-page of a publication in several volumes.

THE WASTE LAND

BY

T. S. ELIOT

FABER & FABER

TWENTY FOUR RUSSELL SQUARE

LONDON

Title-page designed by Mardersteig, relying on impeccable spacing for its effect.

ARAGON
LE CRÈVE-CŒUR

PRÉFACES D'ANDRÉ LABARTHE
ET DE CYRIL CONNOLLY

LONDRES

ÉDITION HORIZON—LA FRANCE LIBRE

1942

Title-page with only a few words, and plenty of white space.

JOHN DONNE
DEAN OF ST. PAUL'S

*

COMPLETE POETRY
AND
SELECTED PROSE

EDITED BY
JOHN HAYWARD

LONDON:
THE NONESUCH LIBRARY
1955

A title-page which uses rules ingeniously.

MONTAGUE WEEKLEY

THOMAS BEWICK

GEOFFREY CUMBERLEGE
OXFORD UNIVERSITY PRESS
LONDON   NEW YORK   TORONTO
1953

A title-page which employs a sizeable illustration as distinct from the device on page 91.

This is, admittedly, only a rough guide for the setting of the title-page, which, in its details, obviously invites great variation in its treatment.

SPACING AND LEADING

Capitals should be letter-spaced, but without exaggeration, and the spacing between letters should never be as much as the amount of white space (leading) between lines.

Letter-spacing undoubtedly enhances the legibility of lines or words of capitals. I M N H U have upright stems, whilst A B C D E F G J K L O P Q R S T V W Z have curved, angular or broken stems. When letters of these two categories come up against each other, awkward gaps of white space or undue cramping are presented to the eye which can be obviated by letter-spacing, e.g.

IRRAWADDY RIVER

not IRRAWADDY RIVER (without letter-spacing).

A title-page contains relatively few lines, and is composed in any case by hand, so the time factor does not press unduly. Thus the letter-spacing can and should be done by hand. This will enable the compositor to do all that is necessary to letter-space correctly the many combinations of capital letters that might occur. The letter I, for instance, needs still more space to the left of it in the combination NI than it does in the combination RI, and so on *ad infinitum*. The above also applies to small capitals.

The leading between lines plays a big part in title-page display. It aids in the throwing of specific words or lines into relief, and is essential between lines of letter-spaced capitals, to enable the capitals to be displayed with the maximum clarity. There should, as we have already remarked, always be more white space between lines than between letters and words. Furthermore, leading affects the 'colour' and balance of the title-page (page 84). De Vinne

A Catalogue of

BOOKS NEWSPAPERS &c.

PRINTED BY

JOHN BELL
b. 1745   d. 1831

OF *THE BRITISH LIBRARY   THE MORNING POST
BELL'S WEEKLY MESSENGER* &c.

AND BY

JOHN BROWNE BELL
b. 1779   d. 1855

SON OF THE ABOVE: FOUNDER OF *BELL'S
NEW WEEKLY MESSENGER   THE NEWS OF THE WORLD*
ETC.

———————————

EXHIBITED AT THE FIRST EDITION CLUB

———————————

𝕷𝖔𝖓𝖉𝖔𝖓

17 BEDFORD SQUARE

15 APRIL—MAY 5

1931

Title-page with ample wording, well leaded and showing
subtle contrasts in type sizes.

has rightly asserted that 'compactness makes confusion. The compositor who sets a title-page will soon learn that it is the relief of white space, as much as the largeness of type, that produces the readability.'

IMPOSITION

We have already discussed the imposition of text pages, and in our illustration on page 34 we have shown that a page opening is an entity. The title-page, on the other hand, is a single right-hand page and thus needs a different imposition.

The top and bottom margins will be uniform with the text pages, but the inner and outer margins will differ from the text in that the inner margin will be increased a little and the outer decreased proportionately.

Occasionally the wording of the title-page will lend itself to a double-spread and in America this has become fashionable. Sometimes an illustration can be incorporated, extending across the two facing pages.

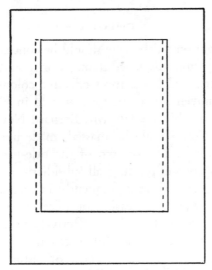

Imposition for title-page.
Dotted lines represent position of text.

SMALL CAPITALS

Small capitals are useful for display on a title-page as an inter-mediate in emphasis between capitals and lower case, and are frequently used for the display of matter subsidiary to the title of the book and the name of the author, such as the details of Preface, Introduction, Translation, number of Illustrations and Volumes, Publisher's Address, etc. Small capitals are, in addition, useful for displaying an extensive array of honours and degrees held by an author, set in a line in a small size below his name.

Hansard held the view that in general 'small capitals are used for the purpose of giving a degree more importance to a word or sentence than would be conveyed by printing the same in italic'. He also reminds us that the small capitals c, o, s, v, w, x and z, so closely resemble the same letters in the lower case, as to require particular care in the composition to prevent their mixing, as the difference can scarcely be discerned but by their being cast on a thicker body than the others.

COLOUR

The use of colour on a title-page should be concentrated and not dispersed over various displayed items; nor should it be used for individual letters. Red is the most effective colour for emphasis and helps to enliven a mass of type printed in black (page 84). Some printers, notably the late Mr. Bernard Newdigate, whilst agreeing that colour should be massed, made use of the process in reverse, printing a line or two of the title-page in black for outstanding display and printing all subsidiary matter in red. He would print in black what is frequently in red, and vice versa. This has certainly proved pleasing on occasions when there is a sufficient number of displayed lines effectively to sustain the black printing. A witty juxtaposition of black and red, or any other appropriate colour, produces an effect of distinction. The same effect may be produced by a solid tint block printed in a pale colour as background for black type (page 83).

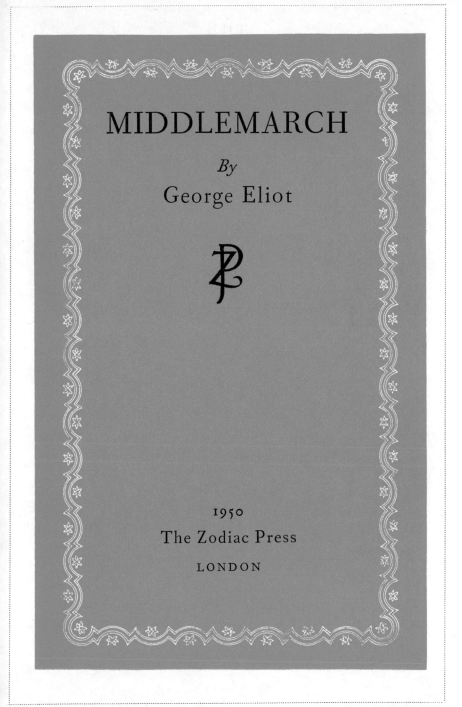

MIDDLEMARCH

By

George Eliot

1950

The Zodiac Press

LONDON

A solid tint makes a good background for a title-page and in this example a border (reversed) is incorporated.

THE

PLEASURES OF

POPE

EDITED

WITH A FOREWORD

BY

PETER QUENNELL

HAMISH HAMILTON

LONDON

Red printing on title-page, more than usually effective because of black printing both
above and below the word in colour.

THE
HOLSTEIN PAPERS

EDITED BY
NORMAN RICH & M. H. FISHER

VOLUME I
*
MEMOIRS
AND
POLITICAL OBSERVATIONS

CAMBRIDGE
AT THE UNIVERSITY PRESS
1955

This title-page has a heraldic decoration connected with the subject
which is neither an illustration nor a publisher's device.

A PROSPECT OF

𝔚ales

—

A SERIES OF WATER-COLOURS
BY KENNETH ROWNTREE
AND AN ESSAY BY
GWYN JONES

PENGUIN BOOKS

LONDON

One word in black-letter can often be very effective.

THE
TWELVE
CAESARS

—

*Gaius Suetonius
Tranquillus*

—

TRANSLATED BY
ROBERT GRAVES

—

Penguin Books

Here a device is turned into a border, wittily emphasizing the title of the book.

Roland Penrose   **Portrait of Picasso**

Published by
Lund Humphries, 12 Bedford Square, London WC1
for the Institute of Contemporary Arts

Picasso: *Self-portrait*. 1904
(Indian ink and water-colour, 6½ × 4).
Col. Dora Maar.

An example of an asymmetrical title-page. Note the deep head margin and the shallow
tail margin.

ORNAMENT

A printer has at his disposal pure typographic ornament in the form of plain rules, swelled rules, flowers, flourishes and ornamental motifs cast in type metal, as well as vignettes which may be available from either wood-engravings or line-blocks. In addition to the above choice of typographic ornament for a title-page, artists are frequently commissioned by the publisher to design special borders or vignettes for the title-pages of specific publications, particularly when the books are illustrated by the same hand.

If ornament is used it should support and not overpower the type matter by its weight of colour, nor should it on the other hand appear weak. The area occupied by ornamentation should not induce a cramped appearance to the type matter; the typesetting must retain its own just proportions and remain easily legible (page 87). Rule work, printers' flowers and other decorative motifs should not be used merely to 'hold together' a poorly composed page.

All rules should be mitred and thus fit perfectly at the corners. Printers' flowers usually have their own special corner pieces; vignettes, including armorial designs and devices, take their place best in the lower half of the page, subsidiary in weight and importance to the title of the book (page 91).

MIXED TYPE FACES

The type face on the title-page is generally that of the text but composed in the various display sizes that are called for. Some of the more skilful printers will introduce, at times, one or more other type faces for emphasis and to impart a degree of decoration. Whilst doing this, it is possible through a judicious choice to retain a visual harmony between the various types, at the same time giving a welcome variety to the page. Indeed, typefounders produce open letters, fully decorative script and plain titling types for use on title-pages (pages 93 and 94).

A CONCISE
ENCYCLOPÆDIA OF GASTRONOMY

SECTION III

VEGETABLES

Comprising an Alphabetical List of Vegetables, Herbs,
Salads, Fungi and edible Weeds, and a selection of
American, English, French, Scottish and
Welsh Recipes for their culinary
preparation and presentation

COMPILED UNDER THE

EDITORIAL DIRECTION OF

ANDRÉ L. SIMON

PUBLISHED BY

THE WINE AND FOOD SOCIETY

28–30 GROSVENOR GARDENS

LONDON, S.W. 1

Title-page showing the main word in a decorative type.

THE
POETICAL WORKS OF
ROBERT
BROWNING

Complete from 1833 to 1868
and the shorter poems **thereafter**

UNIV.
OXONIENSIS

DOM MINA
INUS· TIO·
ILLU MEA

OXFORD UNIVERSITY PRESS
LONDON: HUMPHREY MILFORD

Title-page with well-placed device, harmonizing with the type.

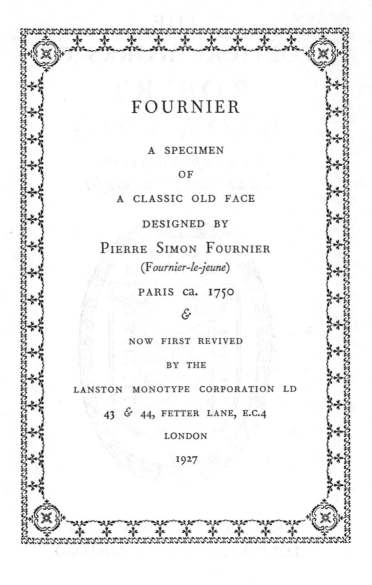

FOURNIER

A SPECIMEN

OF

A CLASSIC OLD FACE

DESIGNED BY

PIERRE SIMON FOURNIER

(*Fournier-le-jeune*)

PARIS ca. 1750

&

NOW FIRST REVIVED

BY THE

LANSTON MONOTYPE CORPORATION LD

43 & 44, FETTER LANE, E.C.4

LONDON

1927

Decorative title-page with border that does not overpower
the type displayed.

FRY'S
ORNAMENTAL

OPEN TITLING

COCHIN OPEN

FOURNIER-LE-JEUNE

ROZAART

DEFGH
IJKL

Historic decorative capitals from the foundry of P. Didot l'Aîné, 19th century, now in the possession of Enschedé of Haarlem.

Decorative types suitable for display of line or word in a title-page.

Moreau~le~Jeune

Union Pearl

𝕭lack 𝕷etter

COLUMNA

GRESHAM

CASTELLAR

JUNO

ORNATA

Decorative types suitable for display of line or word
in a title-page.

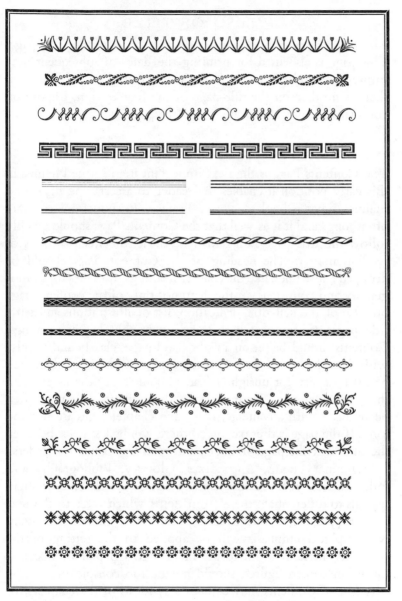

Borders suitable for use on a title-page.

VERSO OF TITLE

The printer's imprint is printed on the verso of the title-page. This page is also used for printing the dates of subsequent new impressions and editions, and the original date of publication if there is no date on the title-page of the first edition. Imposition conforms to that of the title-page (see page 81).

CONTENTS AND LIST OF PLATES

The Contents Page is the next important item in the Prelims. In this early position it enables the reader to ascertain in the easiest manner what a book contains. Preface, Introduction, etc., are often long, and it is as well that the Contents Page should quickly follow the title-page rather than be buried between sections of reading matter. The heading of the Contents Page should be dropped a few lines, like the chapter headings. It makes for homogeneity and consistency if the drop not only of the contents page but also of the half-title, dedication, list of illustrations and part-title pages are uniform with the drop of the chapter openings. Contents should be set on a right-hand page, clearly and simply, with the type leaded. In fact, if the type is well leaded there will be no necessity for unsightly leaders connecting the entry with the page reference. The measure of the contents page may often be reduced with advantage, when the chapter titles are not too long. If the page is thus narrowed there will be less space between the titles and the page numbers, and even less excuse for leaders.

Preliminary items, Appendixes, Glossary, Bibliography and Index entries on the Contents Page can be set in italic or small capitals to differentiate them from items which refer to the text proper (page 97); but whichever course is chosen, the main typographical emphasis will be applied to the setting of the Contents entries relevant to the main text. Chapter numbers, if shown in roman figures, should not be too conspicuous.

A List of Contents may contain a synopsis of the chapters, in which case the chapter number can be centred conveniently above

CONTENTS

Contents page showing titles of chapters set more prominently than the other items. Chapter numbers are ranged on the right and the titles on the left.

(page 99). A List of Illustrations, Plates, Maps or Plans *hors texte* should also be placed on a right-hand page, with the heading ranged with that of the Contents Page. Exception can be made when there are less than, say, six plates or maps, in which case a reference to the illustrations might well be included (if there is space available) as a piece of separate display at the bottom of the Contents Page.

It is not generally necessary to list the illustrations printed in the text; the pagination will show whether a book is complete or not, but with plates *hors texte* there is always a danger of casualties. The List of Plates is, therefore, a guide to what the book should contain.

In a book of two volumes or more, each volume will have its own relevant Contents Page and List of Plates. But the combined index for both volumes will always be placed at the end of the second volume. It is unnecessary to have a Contents Page in a book of fiction when its chapters are merely numbered without chapter titles.

PREFACE AND INTRODUCTION

Both Preface and Introduction open on a recto, with their headings set on the page at the same level as the Contents Page and Chapter Headings. Their head-lines will repeat on the left- and right-hand pages, PREFACE or INTRODUCTION respectively, and need not include the title of the book as in the case of the main text. It is often expedient to introduce some moderate typographical difference between introductory pages and the text. This can be most happily achieved by setting these pages in type a size smaller than that used for the text.[1] If the introductory pages are very brief some printers prefer to set them in italic. But whether the Introduction is set differently from the text or not depends very largely on its nature and length and its exact literary relationship to the text.

[1] Many typographers would not agree with this, and it will help consistency if preface and introduction at least are set in the same size type as the text.—Ed.

CONTENTS

VOLUME I

Contents page with a synopsis for each chapter.

6

APPENDIX, AUTHOR'S NOTES, GLOSSARY BIBLIOGRAPHY AND INDEX

GENERAL

MOST books of any length, exclusive of fiction, children's books, large categories of educational books, Bibles, Prayer Books and the like, require an Index. Books of a scholarly nature frequently contain, in addition, an Appendix, Glossary, Author's Notes and a Bibliography. These sections are paginated in arabic numerals continuing on from the text, and we submit that the headlines on the left-hand and right-hand pages should be the title of the section, e.g. APPENDIX, INDEX, etc. The type for all these subsidiary pages will normally be smaller in size than that of the text.

APPENDIX

The Appendix (plural, Appendixes, except in medical and scientific works when Appendices should be used) starts on a right-hand page, with the heading ranging with the chapter openings of the text. Where there is more than one appendix, each will be clearly numbered, and start on a fresh left- or right-hand page.

AUTHOR'S NOTES

It is most important that the typography of Author's Notes should aid the reader to refer back to a reference in the text. The relevant chapter, page number and actual line on the page should, therefore, be clearly displayed, viz.:

Chapter VIII. Page 99, line 14. *The Advantage of the Woollen Manufacture.* An allusion to the many Acts of Parliament passed in aid of woollen manufactures. The woollen trade of Ireland was destroyed by legislation directed against Irish competition with England.

GLOSSARY

A Glossary has been defined as a 'collection of glosses; list and explanations of abstruse, obsolete, dialectal or technical terms, partial dictionary'. The setting of the glossary is similar to that of a dictionary in so far as each item can readily be referred to.

BIBLIOGRAPHY

The minimum data for entries of a Bibliography comprise title of book, name of author, date and place of publication, and the name of the publisher. The printer should differentiate clearly between the title of the book and the name of the author by the use of italic, capitals, or small capitals for the former. A more full and elaborate Bibliography of the work of an author requires special typographical treatment of a kind suggested below. The double vertical rules indicate each separate displayed line or word as printed on the original title-page.

Seven Poems and a Fragment

1922

SEVEN POEMS AND A FRAGMENT‖ BY WILLIAM BUTLER YEATS ‖ (WOODCUT IN RED) ‖ THE CUALA PRESS ‖ DUNDRUM ‖ MCMXXII

Quarto, size $8\frac{1}{8} \times 5\frac{1}{2}$; pp. xii + 32; price 10/6.

COLLATION: 3 blank leaves; title-page, reverse blank; blank page, on reverse being Table of Contents; blank leaf; text, pp. [1]–24; p. [25] has colophon in red; pp. [26–32] blank.

SIGNATURES: [a] (6 leaves); b to d (3 sheets of 4 leaves); and e (4 leaves). Irish hand-made paper, all edges uncut.

BINDING: dark grey paper boards, light brown linen back, lettered in black on front cover ‖ Seven Poems and a Fragment ‖ By William Butler Yeats ‖. Grey endpapers to match binding.

The edition consisted of 500 copies.

The Press Mark of the British Museum copy is 011649. i. 108.

A full bibliographical setting.

INDEX

A General Index is placed at the end of a book, but there are, in fact, several other forms of Index, e.g. Index of First Lines for Poetry (below), Glossarial Index (page 103), Index to Proper Names, Index to Subjects, etc.

The Index, in whatever form, starts on a recto, and is set in two or more columns unless it is an Index of First Lines. The size of type is generally two sizes smaller than the text. Considerable typographical ingenuity can be exercised in ensuring that the first entry of each alphabetical group is clearly emphasized (pages 103 and 104). The names of books and periodicals should be set in italic, as in the text.

INDEX OF FIRST LINES

A region desolate and wild	*page* 79
A thousand knights have rein'd their steeds	400
A wanderer is man from his birth	195
Affections, Instincts, Principles, and Powers	59
Again I see my bliss at hand	131
And the first grey of morning fill'd the east	198
And you, ye stars	121
Because thou hast believ'd, the wheels of life	59
Before Man parted for this earthly strand	185
Coldly, sadly descends	422
Come, dear children, let us away	80
Come to me in my dreams, and then	130
Creep into thy narrow bed	410
Crouch'd on the pavement close by Belgrave Square	396
Down the Savoy valleys sounding	221
Each on his own strict line we move	129
Even in a palace, life may be led well	397
Far, far from here	112
Far on its rocky knoll descried	404

Index of first lines with white space separating each
alphabetical group.

Jones, Inigo (1573–1652), architect; surveyor-general of works 1615; justice of the peace for Westminster 1630, and for Middlesex; staged many of Jonson's masques, including *Chloridia* (1630–1), 295–8; allusions to, 193; relations with Ben, 295–9, 360, 371–2

Jonson, Ben (1572–1637), his daughter Mary, 8, 351; his son Benjamin, 15, 351; letters from Beaumont, 17, 352; service as a soldier, 40; stay in Hampshire, 48; gratitude to lord d'Aubigny, with whom he lived 1602–7, 48; his ignorance of French, 51; his age, 89, 103; fire at his library, Nov. 1623, 147–53; his studies, 150; the 'Tribe of Ben,' 158–60; his 'sons,' 177; his fat bulk and weight, 103, 165, 167, 168; sues for his pension, 169, 192; his poverty, 167, 169, 172, 182; sickness, 172, 182; his birthday, 11 June, 182; his 'muse,' Venetia Digby, 209; relations with Inigo Jones, *q.v.*, 295–9, 300; his conversations with Drummond, 351–64

Jonson, Benjamin, Ben's 'first sonne'(1596–1603), lines to, 15,351

Jonson, Mary, Ben's daughter, 8, 352

Jonson, William, brother to Ben, 337

Jove, Jupiter, 56, 68, 124, 147, 148, 150, 216, 289

Joves braine, the issue of, Minerva, 124

Jumpe names, names exactly fitting an object, 148

Juno, 38, 94, 295

Justice-hood, alluding to Inigo Jones, *q.v.*, justice of the peace for Westminster and Middlesex, 297

KEmp, William (*fl.* 1600), comic actor in Shakespeare's and Jonson's plays; danced a morris-dance from London to Norwich, described in *Kemps Nine Daies Wonder*, 1600, 52

Kerne, a light-armed Irish footsoldier, 253

Kid, Thomas (1557?–95?), playwright, 243

Kings day, James I's accession-day, 24 March, 153

Kings Evill, scrofula, held to be cured by the royal touch, 172

Kings New Cellar, dedication of, 160

Knat, knot, a bird of the sandpiper kind (*calidris canutus*), 35

LAdy Bess, the princess Elizabeth, *q.v.*, 284

Ladyes' Oak, Penshurst, *q.v.*, 57, 354

Lamia, a vampire who fed on her victim's flesh, 236, 247

Lancelot, Arthurian knight, 149

Langley, perh. Francis Langley, builder and owner of the Swan theatre, Paris Garden, 295

Lanterne-Lerrey, 'some trick of producing artificial light' (Nares); perh. an allusion to Lanthorn Leatherhead, a character in *Bartholomew Fair*, sometimes identified with Inigo Jones, 297

Lapitharum, more (from the fight of the Lapithæ with the Centaurs, cf. Ovid, *Metam.* XII), 304

Lapland, 247

'Lasse, alas, 147

Latin verse, rhyme in, 131

Laura, mistress of Petrarch, *q.v.*, 129

La-ware, Henry, lord De la Warr, *q.v.*, 171

Lay-stall, a common dung-heap, 122

Leave (left) to (stir, etc.), leave (left) off (stirring, etc.), 12, 16, 22, 62, 122

Leda's white Adult'rer, the swan; but it was Cycnus, the son of Sthenelus, who on the banks of Eridanus (*q.v.*) was changed by Apollo

Glossarial Index reproduced from *The Poems of Ben Jonson.*

JAMES I, i, 204; ii, 52
Janin, Jules, i, 373
Jenkinson, v. Stewart
Jerome, St., ii, 256, 382
Jerome of Prague, i, 147
Jerrold, W., ii, 19
Jewel, Bishop, i, 146
John, King of France, ii, 87
Johnson, Lionel, ii, 17
Johnson, Samuel, i, 44, 68, 69; ii,
14, 116, 117, 356; v. Boswell
Jones, Sir William, i, 262
Jonson, Ben, i, 146, 297; ii, 11
Jowett, Benjamin, i, 260
Julian, Emperor, ii, 146, 379

KENT, Earl of, ii, 303
Kilwardley, R., ii, 43

King, Dr. William, i, 269
Kinglake, A. W., i, 258
Kippis, Andrew, i, 121

LAMB, Charles, i, 57; ii, 12, 17;
v. Lamb, 'Letters'
Lami, Giovanni, i, 287
Lang, Andrew, i, 252; ii, 373
Lattini, Brunetto, i, 142
Laurinus, Marcus, ii, 29
Lawrence, Col. T. E., v. Thomas
Le Diable Boiteux, ii, 251

MACAULAY, Lord, i, 271, et seq.,
303, 318, 356; ii, 176; v. Trevelyan
Machiavelli, i, 96, 205
McKinnon, Mr. Justice, ii, 19
Macnaghten, Sir William, i, 392

Index with first words of each alphabetical group
set in small capitals.

J

James I, i, 204; ii, 52
Janin, Jules, i, 373
Jenkinson, v. Stewart
Jerome, St., ii, 256, 382
Jerome of Prague, i, 147
Jerrold, W., ii, 19
Jewel, Bishop, i, 146
John, King of France, ii, 87
Johnson, Lionel, ii, 17
Johnson, Samuel, i, 44, 68, 69; ii,
14, 116, 117, 356; v. Boswell

K

Kent, Earl of, ii, 303
Kilwardley, R., ii, 43
King, Dr. William, i, 269
Kinglake, A. W., i, 258
Kippis, Andrew, i, 121

L

Lamb, Charles, i, 57; ii, 12, 17;
v. Lamb, 'Letters'
Lami, Giovanni, i, 287
Lang, Andrew, i, 252; ii, 373
Lattini, Brunetto, i, 142
Laurinus, Marcus, ii, 29
Lawrence, Col. T. E., v. Thomas
Le Diable Boiteux, ii, 251
Le Gallienne, Richard, ii, 397

M

Macaulay, Lord, i. 271 et seq., 303,
318, 356; ii, 176; v. Trevelyan
Machiavelli, i. 96, 205
McKinnon, Mr. Justice, ii, 19
Macnaghten, Sir William, i, 392
Magliabecchi, i, 161, 196, 287, 290,
409; ii, 397

Index with displayed capital for each alphabetical group.
i and ii refer to the volume numbers.

7

ILLUSTRATION

IT is not our object in this section to describe the various processes available for reproduction;[1] we merely wish to state a few cardinal points. First, for full-page illustrations, we expect the original to be the finest of which each particular artist is capable, regardless of whether it always 'matches' type or not (page 109). Wood, now as always, can most easily be made to harmonize with pages of type (page 107) and, in more recent times, this applies to an even greater degree to the modern line-block whether in colour or in black only. The line-block has been so perfected that brushwork and elaborate pen work can be reproduced, which through excellence of design and contrast to the type often yield a rich result. Such contrast can be further emphasized by Lithography (which has recently undergone a revival), Etchings, Stencils and the Collotype process. In any case, the printing of illustrations is a stimulating challenge to the ingenuity of the printer within the economic limits set by the publisher.

Full-page illustrations of any kind are best printed or guarded in as right-hand pages, since these pages lie flat more easily in an opened book and are thereby the easier to contemplate. Single plates should be securely guarded[2] into the book when binding, plates that are merely tipped in come loose in time. Plates that are grouped together at the end of a book require a half-title between the end of the text and the first plate. Illustrations that are interspersed in the type throughout the text demand processes (line-blocks, wood-engravings or coarse screen half-tone blocks) that can be printed at the same time as the type unless there are special reasons to the contrary. The captions should be set two sizes smaller than the text type, and each caption should bear a number for ready reference when the illustrations are of a documentary

[1] See *Processes of Graphic Reproduction* by Harold Curwen, new ed., 1963.

[2] A counsel of perfection because of the high cost of guarding. If properly tipped in they should be secure for a very long time.—Ed.

	SUNDAY	MONDAY	TUESDAY	WED'SDAY
MAY–JUNE	**30**	**31**	**1**	**2**

REMINDERS

JUNE IN THE KITCHEN GARDEN

Sow kidney-beans, pumpkins, tomatoes, coleworts for a supply of young winter green : under the name of *plants* they are sold nearly all the year round in the London vegetable markets. Cucumbers for pickling, this is indeed the safest and perhaps the best time for sowing this article. *Sow* black Spanish radishes for autumn and winter use, other radishes if wanted, endive principal sowing late in the month. Lettuces, the hardy cosses are now the best to sow, celery for late turnips, peas, cardoons. *Plant* cucumbers and gourds, pumpkins, nasturtiums, and in general similar articles not planted out last month, leeks, celery, cauliflowers, broccoli, borecole, and

Page from *The Gardener's Diary,* with line-block
from a drawing by Edward Bawden.

A BREAST OF VEAL
ROASTED

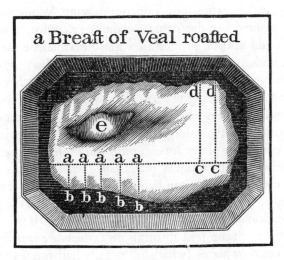

a Breaſt of Veal roaſted

This is the best end of a breast of veal, with the sweet-bread lying on it, and when carved, should be first cut across quite through, in the line a, c, dividing the gristles from the rib-bones: this done, to those who like fat and gristle,

25

Page from *The Art of Carving*
with wood-engraving harmonizing with type.

107

nature. It is not, however, always necessary to list the figures that appear in the text in the List of Illustrations in the preliminary pages as in the case of plates *hors texte*.

It is often necessary to insert tissue paper to protect each plate reproduced by the more delicate and vulnerable processes such as collotype, etching, stencil or copper-engraving. Whilst the caption may be printed on the tissue for quick reference, it is essential that it should also be printed in a more permanent manner, for instance, underneath each plate, as tissues finally become casualties in one way or another in the course of time, either through crumpling or becoming entirely detached from the book.

Where illustrations are grouped together at the end of a book, the half-title page preceding them may be used for printing the order in which the plates appear, with full captions for each item.

It is customary to number plates *hors texte* in roman numerals to avoid confusion with numbered illustrations in the text, and to avoid any possible confusion between the number of the plate and the pagination of the book. Where however there is no difference in kind between the text illustrations (which are usually in line) and the *hors texte* plates (which are usually half-tone) there seems to be no reason for numbering them in separate series.

A common form of illustration is to intersperse decoration throughout the book by the use of headpieces and vignettes, in contrast to full-page designs. In such cases the public expects a book at a moderate price and as it would be uneconomic if the decorative material could not be printed at the same time as the type, wood-engravings or line-blocks are particularly suitable processes for the purpose (page 106).

When blocks are thus embedded in the text it is necessary to leave a space above and below the equivalent of at least one line of type. Placing a block above or below a short line of type should be avoided. Head-lines immediately above the block and page numbers below it should be omitted. Narrow blocks often look better if the type is 'run round' them but this should not be done when their width is more than half the measure because of the difficulty of spacing the short lines of type evenly (page 110).

Je n'ai pas encore assez pavoisé
Le vert et le bleu ont perdu la tête
Tout le paysage est éblouissant
Entre tes deux bras monde sans couleur
Ton corps prend la forme des flammes

A remuer la terre
Et son odeur de rose éteinte
Mains courageuses je travaille
Pour une nuit qui n'est pas la dernière
Mais sûrement la première sans terreurs
Sans ignorance sans fatigue

Une nuit pareille à un jour sans travail
Et sans soucis et sans dégoût
Toute une vie toute la vie
Ecoute-moi bien
Tes deux mains sont aussi chaudes l'une que l'autre
Tu es comme la nature
Sans lendemain

Nous sommes réunis par delà le passé.

57

(Reproduction reduced.)

Page from *Les Yeux Fertiles*
with pen and wash drawing by Picasso
in contrast to the type.

for the roughs were in great force. However, there being no block, not even in Nightingale Lane, he reached the entrance of the wharf, and set down his passenger without annoyance. But as he turned to go back, some idlers, not content with chaffing him, showed a mind to the fare the young woman had given him. They were just pulling him off the box, and Diamond was shouting for the police, when a pale-faced man, in very shabby clothes, but with the look of a gentleman somewhere about him, came up, and making good use of his stick, drove them off.

'Now, my little man,' he said, 'get on while you can. Don't lose any time. This is not a place for you.'

But Diamond was not in the habit of thinking only of himself. He saw that his new friend looked weary, if not ill, and very poor.

'Won't you jump in, sir?' he said. 'I will take you wherever you like.'

'Thank you, my man; but I have no money; so I can't.'

'Oh! I don't want any money. I shall be much happier if you will get in. You have saved me all I had. I owe you a lift, sir.'

'Which way are you going?'

'To Charing Cross; but I don't mind where I go.'

Page from *At the Back of the North Wind* showing type running round the line illustration by Charles Mozley.

8

PAPER, PRESSWORK, BINDING
AND JACKETS

PAPER

PAPER is made in infinite variety to meet the needs of every kind of book, and the right choice of paper for the particular book in hand is obviously of great importance. Type faces that are light in 'colour' demand paper that is more absorbent than the harder papers suitable for the heavier type faces. For instance, Baskerville shows itself to greater perfection on a hard smooth paper, while the lighter-faced Caslon needs the support of a softer, more absorbent paper. Few of our types show to advantage on 'art' shiny paper, but of these, the sturdy Plantin and Times are the most effective. The most suitable kind of paper for the ordinary unillustrated book is one that is flexible, compact, smooth or fairly smooth, pleasant in smell, touch and colour—colour just off-white avoids eye-dazzle. Papers that are thick and flabby should be avoided. Book papers are divided into two distinct categories, namely, laid and wove. Laid papers show intersected wire marks across the sheet, whilst a wove paper presents an even, smooth surface. The laid lines on hand-made paper are a natural result of making paper by hand from a laid mould, which preceded the invention of the wove mould by some centuries. Both laid and wove moulds are in use today in the hand-made paper mills. On the other hand a laid machine-made paper is an anomaly,[1] originating in the attempt to acquire the prestige of a hand-made paper. Wove paper yields the finest results for printing on modern power-driven machines, provided the texture and surface are of the best; indeed, the texture of some of the best and heavier wove papers provides a sufficiency of bulk which is

[1] Laid papers are in fact not often used for bookwork and mould made papers only very seldom.—Ed.

undoubtedly an attraction to publishers. This book, for instance, is printed on a wove paper. All papers should be made so that they can be fed into the machine the right way round, i.e. with the fibres running from top to bottom. This helps to prevent the book from warping when bound and the pages to lie flat when opened. It must be remembered that paper intended for an octavo book should be short grained on the quad sheet, but if it is for a quarto book it should be long grained i.e. the grain should run in the direction of the longer dimension.

Hand-made papers, both wove and laid, should be damped[1] before printing unless they are plate finished, i.e. with a very smooth surface. Deckle edges are naturally produced during the process of making hand-made papers but are entirely artificial in the manufacture of machine-made papers. Deckles collect dirt, particularly on books which are housed in our present-day industrial towns; they are also an inconvenience to the reader in turning over the pages, and even on hand-made papers should be trimmed off. Machine mould-made papers are manufactured from a mixture of rags and sulphite woodpulp, but unlike hand-made papers they should not be damped, as there would be danger of cockling when dry again, owing to the fact that they are not made entirely of rag.

The choice of paper for books with illustrations in the text is, of necessity, conditioned by the kind of illustration and process of reproduction to be used. The choice of paper for plates *hors texte* is usually different from that chosen for the text paper as almost invariably these plates are printed by processes other than letterpress. An approximate match should be arrived at, however, in the colour of the two papers chosen.

PRESSWORK

An essential feature of presswork is the preparation of the impression cylinder and the regulation of the ink so that a regular,

---

[1] Damping is probably never done nowadays because hand-made papers are becoming extinct.—Ed.

even, and crisp impression is obtained over the whole type area. This even impression should sharply define each letter without blurring or under inking. A good black ink is rich and full in colour in its natural state. A cheap black ink is in the end false economy, and tends to produce a black with an unpleasant brown, green or blue tinge. The kind of paper used affects the density of ink required: much less ink for instance is needed when printing on a hand-made paper that has been damped.

BINDING

In England, among other countries, it is the custom to bind or rather to 'case' books in boards. A well-bound book is easy to open and this result is largely achieved by good sewing, accurate case-making, proper casing-in and the use of flexible glue on spine and linings. It is important also that the text paper should be made with the grain running the right way of the fold or else the book will not easily lie open. Endpapers protect the book in the bindery before it is cased and also assist the mull[1] and tapes to hold the book together. They are also a protection against particles of glue or of damp permeating through to the first pages of type matter, and they give a tidiness to the insides of the boards by concealing tapes, mull and 'turnover' of the cloth. Endpapers should therefore be strong and should always be folded and cut with the grain running the right way for the boards; this helps to avoid any warping of the boards after binding. It is only possible to make certain of these conditions if the endpapers are chosen separately from the text paper. Endpapers can also be made effective for a decorative purpose by the application of design or by using patterned or coloured papers.

All bound books should be lettered on the spine with the title and name of the author, so that a book can be instantly identified in its final resting place on the shelves of a library after the jacket

---

[1] Mull is a bookbinder's muslin stiffened and rather easier to use than cambric. It strengthens the joint of back and boards and supplements the holding power of the endpapers.

An exhibit of binding spines, 1930–40.

Left to right: (1) Ink foils. (2) Leather label on buckram. (3) Lithography on cloth. (4) Gold-blocked lettering on leather. (5) Ink foils with lettering blocked in gold. (6) Lithography on cloth. (7 & 8) Lettering and ornamentation blocked in gold on ink foil.

Top: An exhibit of binding spines 1945–1960.
Bottom: This book was published without a jacket.
The lithographed cover was laminated.

has been destroyed or removed. On the other hand, it is unnecessary, except for embellishment, to have lettering on the side of the book, particularly when the book is published complete with a jacket, as the jacket will give all the relevant information as long as the volume is in the bookshop.

Gold leaf still remains the clearest and most permanent material for applying the lettering to the cloth. Ribbon gold is however more generally used today, or foils for imitation-gold or colours. Ink can also be used for the latter. At its simplest brass type can be used but the usual practice is to have lettering drawn for the spine of each individual book. It must be borne in mind that a negative effect, i.e. that of white on black, is produced by the use of gold on a dark cloth, but a positive, i.e. of black on white, if the gold is put on a very light cloth. Such consequences may have little effect on lettering, but can profoundly alter the whole balance of a design or decoration. Allowance must be made for the effect of shading caused by the stamping of the lettering on to binding cloth, which is a yielding material. Though the spine of a book is always a relatively narrow area, it is desirable whenever possible to have the lettering running across (without being too small) rather than running up or down the spine. Drawn lettering can most easily be adapted to economy of space without loss of legibility, and can occasionally be aided by ligatures, e.g.

POOL (type)

POOL (drawn lettering).

An alternative method is to have standard alphabets drawn to serve as models to the brasscutter. Pulls of ordinary type can also be used for this purpose. For those engaged in handling large numbers of different titles, this method has much to commend it (page 118). The brasscutter bears much responsibility, for, whether the lettering is specially drawn or a standard model supplied, he must adjust carefully the letter-spacing and scale of the letters.

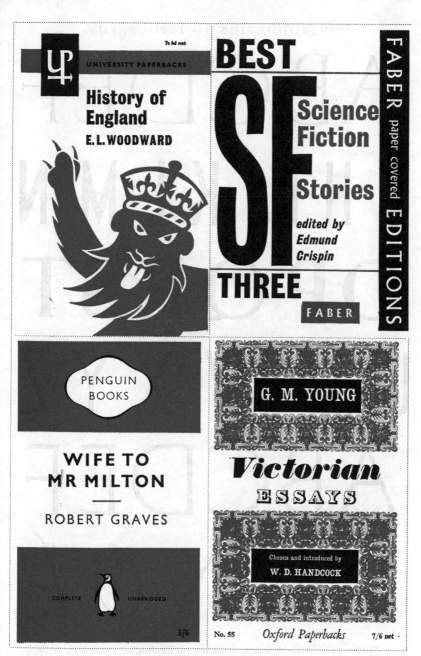

A selection of Paperback covers.

ABCDEF
GHIJKLMN
OPQRST
UVWXYZ
ABCDEF
LMNOP

Portions of alphabets designed for use on bindings. (Jonathan Cape.)

118

The decoration of a bookbinding, at one time an important and often lovely feature, has fallen into neglect especially since book-jackets have played such an important part. Paper-bound books lend themselves, like jackets, to a great variety of treatment, both graphic and typographic, whereas the means of reproducing designs on cloth are very limited. The paper cover fulfils the double function of jacket and cover, but its life is ephemeral; the printed paper cover incorporated in a case (known as a paper case) is frequently used for children's books. Often the jacket design is employed and becomes an integral part of the book.

On page 114 are some examples of designs lithographed on cloth. This is an excellent method of making the jacket design a permanent part of the book.

THE BOOK-JACKET

The last stage of book production is the Book-Jacket. Although extraneous to the book as a whole, it demands the most careful and ingenious treatment. Originally the purpose was mainly protective, but in the course of time it has acquired a potent 'sales' value in addition to its function of supplying in miniature poster form relevant information of title, name of author and publisher. Most books are, as a matter of course, displayed for sale in bookshops both in this country and through export abroad. The book-jacket should appeal to prospective buyers at a first impression, and when there are books displayed of a similar kind but issued by different publishers, the excellence of the jacket will play a competitive part.

The approach to designing a book-jacket is more simple in some kinds of books than others. Books on more scholarly and specialized subjects, which do not lend themselves to ordinary methods of salesmanship, can well have jackets in a typographic style tending to harmonize with the typography of the book itself. Again, jackets for a standard library such as *Everyman*, where new titles are added from year to year, must have a recognizable style which will remain inviting over a long period.

It is in the more general and highly competitive field that the jacket presents its greatest demand for novelty and difference from its fellows. Great variety can, of course, be achieved by employing different processes for different kinds of designs. Where work has been specially commissioned from artists, lithography, four-colour half-tone work, and the line-block (in colours or black only) may be used for reproduction; the choice of any one of these processes will depend on the nature of the original design. When a photograph is to be reproduced, either a half-tone block, photo offset or photogravure is necessary.

The most economic and not the least effective is the purely typographic jacket. Typefounders offer a large number of display borders and faces of the requisite weight and carrying power for the setting of jackets (pages 121 and 122). By the skilful use of this wealth of material, it should be possible to achieve effects which will at the same time attract the attention of buyers standing some distance from the bookshop window or shelf, and yet be agreeable when the book is actually in the hand. We should not infer that all jackets should be bold in their type-setting; on the contrary, variety is essential and this can be achieved in many ways by displays ranging from the simple to the ornate, in conjunction with variety in colour of inks and colour of papers. Many publishers produce books with certain similarities of style running through the jacket designs of most of their publications with the object of making their own publications recognizable by the book-buying public.

When publisher and printer are able to work exceptionally closely together, it is possible to assist the display by the kind of wording or 'blurb' supplied (page 124). This blurb may at times be an integral part of the typographic design on the front of a jacket, supplementary to the displayed words of title and author. The spine of a jacket, although narrow in relation to the side, should not be neglected; many books are displayed showing their spines only. When the area is sufficient for a continuation of an attractive display, the opportunity should not be neglected (page 125).

ALBERTUS

CHISEL

FAT FACE

PROFIL

Headline Bold

Echo

Hyperion

PLAYBILL

Ashley Script

Display types suitable for jackets.

ORPLID **ARPKE**

THORNE SHADED

ULTRA BODONI

ELONGATED ROMAN

TIMES HEAVY TITLING

ULTRA BODONI CONDENSED

TEA-CHEST

GILL SANS BOLD

SANS SERIF SHADOW LINE

SANS SERIF SHADED

KLANG

Display types suitable for jackets.

122

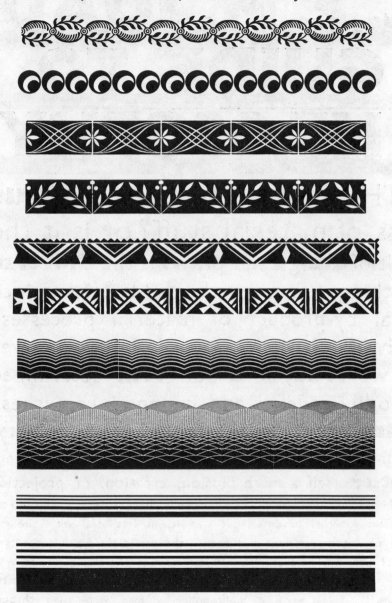

Borders suitable for jacket display.

C. E. M. JOAD

GUIDE TO

PHILOSOPHY

IS THE **Universe** a **fortuitous** mass of material stuff? or is it the result of **design** and **plan?** Is the **Universe** one thing — or many things? Is **Life** an incidental by-product of material processes? Is **Evolution** haphazard or purposive? Are we **Free,** or is our **Will** determined by bodily reflexes and unconscious wishes? Is **Mind** a unique and independent activity, or a mere function of bodily processes? Alternatively, is **Matter** itself a mere illusion, creation, or projection of mind? Is the human mind an instrument fitted to give us knowledge of a world external to ourselves? Can it, in fact, deal with the raw material of reality, or must it " cook " the world, before it consents to know it? Can we, in short, discern anything in the world except what our minds have first put there, and is the philosopher a man who fares through the confines of the universe to discover himself?

592 pp ● 7/6

Jacket showing varied typographic treatment of 'blurb'.

ADVICE TO A PROPHET RICHARD WILBUR

RICHARD WILBUR

ADVICE TO A PROPHET

Faber

Front and spine of jacket which makes effective
use of heavy rules.

THE OUTSIDER

with an introduction by
CYRIL CONNOLLY

ALBERT CAMUS

Awarded the Nobel Prize for Literature

Front of jacket, straightforward and bold typographical treatment
making full use of coloured ink.

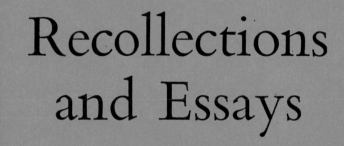

RECOL-
LECTIONS
AND
ESSAYS
✦
LEO
TOLSTOY

459

THE
WORLD'S
CLASSICS

LEO TOLSTOY

Recollections and Essays

OXFORD

One of a series, the jackets of which avoid uniformity
and too great a diversity at the same time.

An
Introduction to
POSITIVE
ECONOMICS

Richard G.
Lipsey

An Introduction to
POSITIVE
ECONOMICS

Richard G. Lipsey

*Professor of Economics at the
London School of Economics*

Weidenfeld
& Nicolson

Red is used sparingly but effectively here.

COLLECTED POEMS | JOHN LEHMANN

COLLECTED POEMS

JOHN LEHMANN

E & S

This jacket gets its effect not from the size of type used
but from the white space all round it.

MISCELLANEOUS

SWASH LETTERS

SWASH capitals are a set of letters supplementary to certain italic capital letters for use at the beginning and sometimes at the end of words in displayed lines. Swash letters are, in fact, in the nature of an exuberant flourish (swell letter), decorative in effect, which had its origin in the scriptorium. Whilst swash capital letters can be used for chapter openings and on the various preliminary pages, and even on rare occasions on headlines, it is on a title-page that they can most fully be brought into play.

Swash capital letters need careful and consequently slow composition, the letters being inserted by hand and meticulously spaced. The kerns are delicate and are inclined to break, and a vigilant watch must be kept throughout all stages of production to avoid broken letters.

Any display incorporating swash letters should be kept within the bounds of reticence; their too frequent use would quickly become tiresome; and only when they are used in moderation can the element of surprise and fancy be maintained.

NEW BRUNSWICK

not

NEW BRUNSWICK

The Black Prince (plain)   *The Black Prince* (swash)

Examples of Caslon swash capital letters in use.

Of the twenty-three type faces shown on pages 14–17, few are supplied with swash letters. Only Caslon italic and Garamond italic (page 131) are thus fully equipped in capitals.

A B C D E G F K M
N P R T U Y

Caslon swash capitals.

A B C D E G L M
N P R T

Garamond swash capitals.

SWASH LOWER-CASE ITALIC LETTERS

The principles governing the use of swash lower-case letters are similar to those governing swash capitals, but more frequently they will be used only as terminal letters to displayed words set in capitals and lower-case italic.

As in the case of capitals few founts are provided with swash lower-case letters, Caslon and Garamond italic each have them. With Garamond the Monotype Corporation provides a generous supply of ligatures and logotypes.

b k v w

heliotrope, white & vermilion (plain)

heliotrope, white & vermilion (swash)

trowel not *trowel*

Caslon lower-case swash letters.

Ex Na Ne Ni No Nu Qu Ra Re Ri Ro Ru
q₃ gg gy ꝫ m nt ta v ſa ſb ſc ſe ſh ſi ſl ſk ſo ſu ſs ſt ſæ ſſa ſſe ſſi
ſſo ſſu ſ ſſ ſs ſt ct as fr is k ll ſp tt us zy

Garamond ligatures, logotypes and swash letters.

131

BRACKETS AND SWELLED RULES

We have already referred to the primary use of brackets in the section of Rules of Composition (see page 4), but they can be enlisted for other purposes. To some eyes, pages that for various reasons are without head-lines look unduly spartan; this is relieved when the pagination is set within brackets, thereby giving a suggestion of ornamentation. In the setting of plays, the square bracket is available for several minor functions (pages 61 and 62), whilst in poetry, when the poems themselves are numbered rather than titled, the setting of the pagination in brackets will clearly make sufficient difference between the two sets of numerals appearing on the same page (page 133).

Miss Peggy Lang has drawn attention to the value of the swelled rule as an element of design and as a means of focusing the eye on the vertical centre of the page. She defines the scope of the swelled rule well when she says: 'It signifies hiatus rather than separation or finality. While its weight achieves emphasis, the tapering ends prevent obtrusiveness, and by its own graduation it brings into harmony varying weights of type. It lends shape to the traditional title-page and helps to overcome the bareness normally attending the short modern title. A single rule, or pair, emphasizes and adorns chapter headings, while a shorter dash signifies pause at the ends of sections.'[1]

Swelled rules are supplied by typefounders both in their simple and decorative forms (page 134). As with swash letters, their employment can easily become tiresome if overdone, and their use by unskilled hands can bring much ugliness to the printed page. A well-selected decorative swelled rule can impart as much beauty to a page as a vignette or printer's flowers. But when the swelled rule is of the simpler, plain sort, whether used for decoration or for some specific purpose, it should be finely tapered. The ultra-fat sort invariably annoys the reader and rarely justifies itself for use with text or display types used in books.

[1] 'Swelled Rules and Typographical Flourishes', by Peggy Lang. *Signature* No. 9. 1938.

193

The tender bud within herself doth close
With secret sweetness till it prove a rose;
And then as fit for profit as for pleasure
Yields sweet content to him that gains the treasure:
 So she that sent this, yet a bud unblown,
 In time may prove a rose, and be your own.

194

While o'er the Globe, fair Nymph! your searches run,
And traced its rolling circuit round the sun,
You seemed the world beneath you to survey
With eyes ordained to give its people day;
With two fair lamps methought your nations shone,
While ours are poorly lighted up by one.
How did those rays your happier empire gild!
How clothe the flowery mead and fruitful field!
Your earth was in eternal spring arrayed,
And laughing Joy amidst its natives played.

Such is their day, but cheerless is their night,
No friendly moon reflects your absent light:
And oh! when yet ere many years are past
Those beams on other objects shall be placed,
When some young hero with resistless art
Shall draw those eyes and warm that virgin heart,
How shall your creatures then their loss deplore,
And want those suns that rise for them no more!
The bliss you give will be confined to one,
And for his sake your world must be undone.

195

I've wandered east, I've wandered west,
 Through mony a weary way;
But never, never can forget
 The luve o' life's young day!
The fire that's blawn on Beltane e'en,
 May weel be black gin Yule;
But blacker fa' awaits the heart
 Where first fond luve grows cule.

Page showing numbered poems, with pagination in brackets.

PLAIN SWELLED RULES

DECORATIVE SWELLED RULES

Monotype

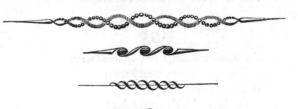

Designed by Berthold Wolpe for the Fanfare Press

Engraved by Reynolds Stone for The Curwen Press

Engraved by Joan Hassall for The Curwen Press

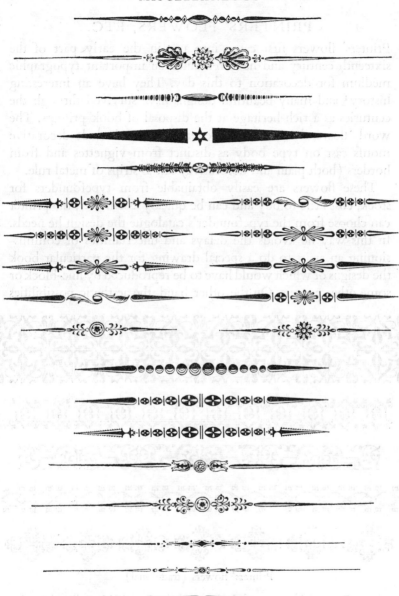

A collection of Victorian decorative swelled rules in use at the Westerham Press.

PRINTERS' FLOWERS, ETC.

Printers' flowers first came into use in the early part of the sixteenth century and have remained an important typographic medium for decoration to this day. They have an interesting history[1] and many beautiful designs have survived through the centuries as a rich heritage at the disposal of book printers. The word 'flowers' is used as a general term to include decorative motifs cast on type body as distinct from vignettes and from borders (both plain and decorative) cast as strips of metal rule.

These flowers are easily obtainable from typefounders for stock, cost little to buy and can be quickly assembled; the printer can choose from the typefounder's catalogue the design he needs. In this way he avoids the delays and uncertainties of commissioning an artist to do a special drawing for the particular book the designs of which would have to be reproduced by line-block or some other process. On the other hand, the aesthetic possibilities

Printers' flowers (traditional).

[1] See 'Printers' Flowers and Arabesques', by Francis Meynell and Stanley Morison. *The Fleuron,* No. 1. 1923.

of flowers are to a certain extent limited, and there is a danger of tiring the public through a too-constant repetition of the same motif, for typefounders' flowers are available to every printer in the land. This objection would be countered if more printers were to commission new designs which would become the possession, through copyright, of their own particular press. Proprietary type, which was common enough before the industrial era, is hardly practical today, but proprietary flowers remain a suitable field for a printer's initiative. He can thus acquire something different from anything a typefounder can offer, and for a moderate outlay. It is no easy undertaking to design a flower complete with corner pieces which can be repeated in a variety of built-up patterns. It is still more difficult to produce a design which, satisfactory as a single unit or a composite motif, shows itself equally effective in a built-up pattern with other units or motifs, whether the printing is in black only or in black and colour. Built-up designs of printers' flowers can be assembled in a great variety of subtle combinations which can be further enriched by the use of colour in the printing. In addition to 'flowers' there is a great variety of ornamental motifs cast in type metal available to printers for independent use or in combination with rules and decorative borders.

Composite rule and flower borders.

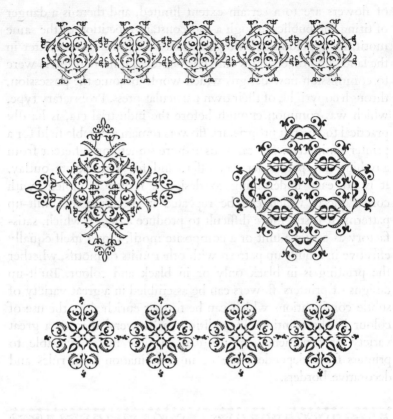

Single motifs used in combinations above.

Built-up flower patterns.

This frame is composed of the above Monotype units.

NUMERALS

Roman numerals were used by the earliest fifteenth-century printers because they had no arabic figures. Even today they are sometimes employed, but for special purposes such as the pagination of preliminary pages, for use on chapter headings (see page 49) and for the designation of part numbers, appendixes, etc. They are, too, useful for numbering plates inserted as illustrations *hors texte* (see page 108). Nevertheless they are not quickly interpreted and, while we are all at our ease up to XII through our familiarity with the clock face, the higher numerals require a considerable amount of mental calculation. Those in most frequent use are made up of a combination of the seven capitals I, V, X, L, C, D and M. Any letter, or letters, representing a number of low value which follows a letter of high value must be added to its value and any letter or letters preceding such a number must be subtracted from its value.

1=I	12=XII	50=L	700=DCC
2=II	13=XIII	60=LX	800=DCCC
3=III	14=XIV	70=LXX	900=CM
4=IV	15=XV	80=LXXX	1000=M
5=V	16=XVI	90=XC	1500=MD
6=VI	17=XVII	100=C	1700=MDCC
7=VII	18=XVIII	200=CC	1800=MDCCC
8=VIII	19=XIX	300=CCC	1895=MDCCCXCV
9=IX	20=XX	400=CD	1900=MCM
10=X	30=XXX	500=D	1944=MCMXLIV
11=XI	40=XL	600=DC	2000=MM

Arabic numerals do not present any difficulties to the reader, and today their general use is greater than ever in catalogues, bibliographies, for chapter headings, and on title-pages. This has come about through more and more founts of type being issued with both old style and modern arabic numerals in roman and sometimes in italic as well. This gives to arabic numerals a remarkable degree of flexibility.

1 2 3 4 5 6 7 8 9 0
Modern

1 2 3 4 5 6 7 8 9 0
Old Style

1 2 3 4 5 6 7 8 9 0
Modern Italic

1 2 3 4 5 6 7 8 9 0
Old Style Italic

1 2 3 4 5 6 7 8 9 0
Bold

Walbaum numerals.

Modern numerals range with the capitals of the fount, viz. CHAPTER 25. Old style numerals are less assertive and are designed for use for dates, measurements, etc., in the text and for tabular work. They can also be used ranged with small capitals, viz. CHAPTER 25. Old style numerals are relatively unobtrusive because of the variation of their ranging on the centre of their axis.

1, 2 and 0 range with and are the same size as the lower-case letters a, c, e, etc.

3, 4, 5, 7, and 9 range with and are the same depth as the lower-case letters with descenders g, j, p, q and y.

6 and 8 range with and are the same height as the lower-case letters with ascenders b, d, f, h, k and l, and generally range with capitals as well.

When a fount contains modern and old style numerals, the use of both may be called for in the same book—modern for the numbering of chapters, old style for numerals in the text, pagination and the dates on the title and verso. These two varieties are particularly useful for bibliographies and catalogues—modern for the item number followed by displayed capitals—the less obtrusive old style for dates and measurements (page 143). The unequal range of old style numerals is most convenient for tabular work where there are solid masses of figures. The eye can pick out each item more easily than would be the case if all numerals presented a solid ranged mass.

For comprehensive instructions as to the proper usage of figures and numerals we refer our readers to *Rules for Compositors and Readers* (Oxford University Press).

19 LEPRIEUR, A. (attributed to) *Inches*

A French immigrant artist working in England
about 1745–1760. The few other pictures attributed
to him represent Thames-side scenes

INN BY A POOL 32×58

Lent by Colonel M. H. Grant

20 LOUTHERBOURG, P. J., R.A., 1740–1812

Born at Strasbourg, came to England in 1771, and
became celebrated as a painter of 'picturesque' landscapes, coast scenes, etc.

THE MILKMAID 20×28

(closely resembles Ibbetson in style)

Lent by Colonel M. H. Grant

21 MANSKIRK, F. J., 1770–1827

A German artist. He came to England about 1793
and painted landscapes of park and garden scenes

CHEPSTOW AND THE WYE 27×32

Exhibited at the Royal Academy, 1799

Lent by Colonel M. H. Grant

22 MARLOW, W., 1740–1813

Pupil, but not an imitator, of Samuel Scott. Painted
many views of country seats, bridges, etc., both in
oil and water-colour

RICHMOND BRIDGE 25½×36

Signed

Lent by Colonel M. H. Grant

23 MORLAND, G., 1763–1804

Celebrated painter of landscapes with figures and
animals, coast and fishing scenes, etc.

LANDSCAPE: SANDHILLS WITH FIGURES

Lent by Lionel W. Neeld, Esq. Panel 16×20½

Page from a catalogue showing use of modern numerals ranged with the
displayed capitals. Old style numerals are used for dates and measurements.

GLOSSARY

Ampersand: The name given to the contraction of 'and', thus: &.

Antiqua: The German name for roman type.

Antique paper: A term used to describe any good book paper with a rough surface.

Art paper: A clay-coated paper, especially suitable for half-tone block printing. This is generally produced with a highly glazed surface but when the surface is matt it is known as matt art paper.

Author's proof: A proof showing corrections made by the author or editor; any departures from MS. after proofing are made at the customer's expense.

Back-up: To print the reverse side of a sheet when one side is already printed, also termed 'perfecting'.

Backs: The back margins of pages, those which adjoin the binding.

Beard: The blank metal sloping away from the actual face of a letter, at its head and foot. Depth of beard varies considerably on different types, and it is often necessary in large sizes to trim the beard in order to obtain closer line spacing.

Binder's brass: A brass block cut especially deep for blocking on cloth bindings.

Black letter: A term loosely covering Old English or Gothic Text.

Bleed: Illustrated books are said to have 'bled edges' when the final trim cuts into the illustrations or background tints. Allowance for this 'bleed off' is made beforehand by making the blocks over-size. If the book is illustrated by drawings the artist should extend his drawing in such a way that it will not be spoilt when it is slightly cut into. This description is also used occasionally on 'non-bled' work, to indicate mutilation by over-cutting.

Blind blocking: The blank impression made by a binder's brass block on a cloth binding, i.e. with no ink or foil.

Blocks: A general term which covers line-blocks, half-tones, electros, etc.

Body: The solid shank of the letter. Size of body, i.e. measurement from back to front, is constant throughout any single fount.

Body of the work: The text proper of a volume, as distinct from preliminary pages, indexes and appendixes, etc.

Bold face: A heavy type, frequently used in contrast with types of ordinary weight or colour. Many type faces have their own bold face, i.e. type of the same design, but in a heavier version.

Bolts: The folded edges at the head, tail and fore-edge of a printed sheet before trimming.

Bowl: Any curved main-stroke of a letter surrounding a closed 'white', or counter.

Bulk: The thickness of a book. Short books can be made fat by means of 'bulky' papers, the most extreme and objectionable being known as featherweights.

Calendered paper: Highly glazed paper, so called because the polished finish is given by a stack of cylinders called 'calenders'.

Cancel: A new leaf or leaves reprinted to rectify some error or defect.

Capitals: CAPITALS. Abbreviated to caps. and indicated in manuscript by three underlinings of the words to be thus set.

Captions: Descriptive matter, usually short, placed beneath illustrations. Also known as 'legends'.

Cartridge paper: A hard, tough class of paper made with a rough surface in many grades. Particularly useful for drawing.

Case: In hand composition, a shallow wooden tray to hold type, divided into compartments to take the various letters of the alphabet. The arrangement is standard for all types and sizes. In binding, a case is the made-up cover, ready for affixing to the trimmed book.

Cast-off: The preliminary measurement of a manuscript to form an estimate of the number of pages required of a given size of type and area.

Catchline: A temporary descriptive headline on proofs. Also the name given to a short line of type in between two large displayed lines.

Chase: A metal frame, made of wrought iron or steel, into which type is locked, ready for printing.

Clean proof: A proof absolutely correct according to the 'copy' or manuscript.

Coated paper: Another name for art paper.

Cockling: In paper, cockling, a bumpy and uneven condition, may be caused by exposure to damp or uneven heat.

Collating: After the various printed sections of a work are gathered they are checked by means of collating marks on the spine to make sure they are in the right order. This is known as collating.

Collotype: A photo-mechanical non-screen process in which printing is done from a gelatine film, slightly below the surface.

Colophon: An inscription at the end of a book often including the printer's imprint and a note of details of production.

Composing stick: An adjustable metal or wooden hand tray for receiving lines of movable type as they are set. This is used in conjunction with a setting rule, which keeps each line distinct from the last while setting.

Condensed face: Thin, elongated type, useful for long words which are to be displayed in a narrow space.

Contents page: A page included in the preliminary pages of a book giving a list of contents and occasionally a list of illustrations.

Copy: Any matter to be set in type.

Counter: The interior 'white' of a letter. It may be completely enclosed as in O or partly enclosed as in E.

Cropping: Work that has been cut down too much is said to have been 'cropped'.

Crown: A standard size of printing paper measuring 15″ × 20″. A sheet 20″ × 30″ is known as Double Crown, while Crown Folio, Crown Quarto (Cr. 4to) and Crown Octavo (Cr. 8vo) are half size, quarter size and one-eighth of Crown respectively.

Cursive: The German name Kursiv, for italic types.

Cut: A trade term (American) for illustrations of any kind in the text.

Day (Ben) mediums: 'Mechanical' tints. These are standard designs used on line-blocks to give degrees of tone and texture. They are put down on the zinc from celluloid screens.

Deckle: The name given to the uneven, rough edges of hand-made paper.

Demy: A standard size of printing paper measuring $17\frac{1}{2}'' \times 22\frac{1}{2}''$.

Display work: A term applied to the setting of short lines in varying faces and sizes of type, as distinct from a solid block of type. Advertisements, titles and headings are 'display' work.

Distribution of type: The operation of melting type down or returning it to case after printing, when the type need no longer be kept standing. This is known as 'dis.'.

Double-spread: Two facing pages containing matter which is continuous across both pages.

Drawn-on covers: A form of binding square-backed magazines and books in paper covers. The cover is attached by glueing to the back of the book.

Dropped heads: A name given to chapter headings which are driven down from the top of the page.

Dummy: A sample copy of the proposed work made up before printing with the actual materials, i.e. paper and covers, and cut to the correct size to show bulk, style of binding, etc. A dummy usually contains a specimen printed page to show suggested type and is useful for estimating costs.

Electronic scanning and engraving: This is the latest method of colour separation and engraving which can be used in conjunction with either letterpress printing or lithography.

Electrotype: A printing plate made by electrolytically depositing copper on to a mould of wax or lead taken from an original plate or from type, and backed with a lead alloy.

Em: The square of any size of type. Also the name given to the printer's general measure, 12 points, or one-sixth of an inch. This 12-pt. em is the standard for measuring the depth and width of a page.

En: Half an em in any size of type. It is the average width of the letters in a fount and is a useful basis for calculation.

Endpapers: The leaves at the beginning and end of a book, the first and last of which are pasted on to the binding. Endpapers are often decorated, or are sometimes of another colour.

Even working: See Oddment.

Face of a type: The printing surface of any letter.

Figure: A line block printed with the text as distinct from a plate. Called 'cut' in America.

Finishing: A binder's term for the lettering and decoration of the case.

First proof: The first pull of a setting after composing which is read from 'copy', after which it is corrected and reproofed as a 'clean' proof.

Flong: Sheets of prepared papier mâché used for making moulds, or matrices, in stereotyping.

Flowers: Decorative motifs cast in metal to type sizes which may be made up into ornaments or borders. Also called fleuron.

Folio: This term when following a paper size signifies half a sheet of that size. A page number is often referred to as a folio.

Foolscap: A standard size of printing paper measuring $13\frac{1}{2}'' \times 17''$.

Footnotes: Notes at the foot of the page, but still contained within the type area, and set in a size two points smaller than the text size. A line of white usually separates the text from the footnote.

Fore-edge: The edge of a book opposite the binding, i.e. the front edge, as distinct from head and tail.

Format: A covering term for the size and shape of a book.

Forme: The combination of chase, furniture and type locked up for machine, i.e. the pages imposed in a chase.

Forwarding: All work done by the binder after sewing, including the casing of the book.

Fount: A complete set of any particular type comprising letters, figures and punctuation marks, etc. The quantities supplied of each character vary in accordance with general needs.

Frame: A rack containing type cases at which the compositor works.

French-fold: A sheet of paper with four pages printed on one side only and folded into four without cutting the head. The inside of the sheet is therefore completely blank.

Frontispiece: The illustration facing the title-page of a book.

Full point: A printer's term for a full stop.

Furniture: Wood or metal used to fill in the blank spaces in a forme around and between the pages of type, all held together in the chase.

Galley: A metal tray in which type is placed when composed, before making up into pages. 'Galley-proofs' are proofs pulled from the type contained in these galleys.

Gathering: Placing the sections of a book in their correct order before binding.

Grotesque: The name given to the earliest sans-serif types.

Guarded in: A term used to describe plates which are inserted into a book without being pasted in the ordinary way. The paper area of the plate is wider than the book page, and the projecting part is wrapped round the back of the section and a narrow strip of paper consequently appears elsewhere in the back of the book.

Gutter: The bookbinder uses the word 'gutter' for the back margin of a book: also an imposition term and applies to the space comprising the fore-edges of pages, plus the trim, where these fore-edges fall internally in the forme.

Hair spaces: Very thin inter-letter and inter-word spaces, equal to $\frac{1}{12}$ of the body width in the middle ranges of a fount series, but varying for very small and larger sizes, thus in 6 pt. the hair space is $\frac{1}{2}$ pt.; in 12 pt. it is $1\frac{1}{2}$ pts.; in 18 pt. it is 2 pts.; and in 24 pt. it is 3 pts.

Half bound: A style of binding having the back and corners covered in a different material from that which covers the sides.

Half-tone block: A printing plate of copper or zinc, photographically produced with the aid of a mechanically ruled screen which reduces the image to a series of dots varying in density according to the tone values of the original.

Hand-made paper: Very durable paper made in individual sheets, by a moulding tray being dipped into a pulp composed of linen rag fibres.

Heads: The head margins of a book.

Headpiece: Decoration at the beginning of a chapter.

Imperfection note: The binder's list of shortages encountered when he has reached the end of an edition. Certain signatures or plates may be missing because of spoilage or short printing and it is customary to print the requisite extra copies of these when the book is reprinted.

Imposing surface: Known as the 'stone'. A flat surface, usually of metal, on which pages of type are imposed and locked up in chase for printing.

Imposition: The laying-down of pages in position for printing, in such a way as to ensure correct sequence when printed and folded.

Imprint: This is the few lines appearing in printed works, which give the name and address of the printer. It is required by an Act of Parliament.

Indent: To begin a line with a blank space, thus setting the line back a little, for instance, the first line of a new paragraph is usually indented.

India paper: A very thin, strong, opaque paper made of rag, used for Bible printing and such other works as require a great many pages in a small bulk.

Initial letters: Large capital letters, often decorative, frequently used at the beginning of a work and sometimes at the beginning of each chapter. Initial letters may be dropped, so that the top of the letter ranges with the top of the first line of text, or raised so that the bottom of the initial letter ranges with the bottom of the first line of text.

Inner forme: The pages of type which fall on the inside of a sheet: this is the reverse of the 'outer' forme.

Inset: A sheet or part of a sheet placed inside another sheet after folding in order to complete the sequence of pagination for that section. A loose sheet placed inside a book or booklet is also known as an inset.

Intertype: A slug-setting machine.

Justification: The name given to the equal and exact spacing of words and letters to a given measure. This is done in mechanical setting as well as by hand.

Kern: This is any part of the face of a letter which extends over the edge of the body and rests on the shoulder of the adjacent letter.

Key: The block or forme in letterpress printing, and the plate or stone in lithography, which acts as guide for position and registration of the other colours.

Laid paper: Paper which shows parallel wire marks, 'laid lines', due to its manufacture on a mould in which the wires are laid side by side.

Lay edges: The edges of a sheet of paper which are laid against the front and side lay gauges of a printing or folding machine. The front lay edge is the 'gripper edge'.

Lay-out: The preparation of copy for setting, with an indication of the type to be used, the type area and the position of blocks, etc., on the page.

Leads: Strips of lead, less than type high, used for spacing out lines of type. They are made to given point thicknesses as follows: 1 pt., 1½ pt. or thin lead, 2 pt. or middle, 3 pt. or thick lead.

Leaf: A 'sheet' of a book which is printed both sides and is equal to two pages.

Leaders: Rows of dots used to guide the eye across the page, often used in tabular work.

Letterpress: Printing from raised type or blocks, as distinct from lithographic, or plate printing.

Letter-spacing: Spacing placed between the letters of a word.

Ligatures: Tied letters, such as fi, ff, fl, etc., cast on one body, to avoid unsightly juxtaposition of fi, ff, fl, etc., and to lessen the risk of damage to kerned letters. Ligatures derive from the early days of printing when letters were cut to resemble formal handwriting.

Line-block: A printing plate of zinc, or occasionally copper, produced photographically and chemically, from which may be printed a reproduction of any line ('black and white') drawing.

Linotype: A composing machine of American origin which sets matter in solid lines or 'slugs'. Used in Britain chiefly for newspaper-work and in America extensively for bookwork.

Literals: Errors made by the printer in setting up type from MS.

Lithography: Printing from a porous stone or zinc plate. A plano-graphic process.

Lower case: Letters which are not capitals, thus: a, b, c; also the name given to the case which holds these letters.

Make-ready: The detailed preparation before printing a forme. It includes underlaying and overlaying to overcome inequalities in type and to ensure an impression of proper strength on every part of the printing area.

Make-up: To take type from the galley and arrange in pages to a given depth. In book and magazine work, 'make-up' is the instructions given to the printer for the arrangement of matter and illustrations on each page.

Margins: The white space surrounding a page of printed type.

Marginal notes: Annotations which appear in the side margins of a page. Also called 'side-notes' and 'hanging shoulder notes'.

Matrix: A copper mould into which the image has been struck by a punch, used for casting type. A matrix exists for each character in each fount of type. A papier-mâché mould used in stereo-typing is also called a matrix.

Measure: This is the width to which type is set and it is always a stated number of 12-pt. ems.

Medium: A standard size of paper measuring 18″ × 23″.

M.F.: Machine Finished. Describes the surface (varying according to requirements) put upon paper while actually in the machine.

M.G.: Machine Glazed. A class of papers rough on one side and glazed on the other. Used for posters, wrappings, etc.

Modern: A general descriptive term for those type faces which show a characteristic vertical emphasis and fine, bracketed hair-serifs.

Monotype: A composing machine of American origin which casts single types. Generally used in bookwork.

Mould-made paper: A machine-made substitute for hand-made paper.

Nick: A groove appearing in the shank of every piece of type which acts as a guide to the compositor in setting the type the right way up.

Nonpareil: A name given to a 6-pt. lead. The term derives from the name formerly given to a type of 6 pts. in size.

Nut quad: A term for an en quadrat.

Octavo: The size of a sheet of paper when folded into eight. Abbreviated to 8vo.

Oddment: When the pages of a book make an exact multiple of sixteen (or of thirty-two if it is being sewn in 32-page sections) it is said to make an even working. Any pages extra are said to be oddments.

Offcut: When a work is printed in an odd size, i.e. not conforming to standard paper sizes, there is very often a surplus piece on the printing paper which is trimmed off. This is known as an offcut.

Offset printing: A process of printing in which the image is transferred from a lithographic plate to a rubber roller which is pressed on to the printing paper. This method now so generally used that offset has become a synonym for lithography.

Old Face: Those type faces characterized by oblique emphasis, lightness of colour, comparatively small differences between the thick and thin strokes and fairly substantial bracketed serifs, of which the first complete series was cut in France, *c.* 1535. There are many modern revivals of Old Faces, notably Caslon, Bembo and Garamond.

Opening: Two facing pages of a book.

Overlays: These are used in 'making ready' an illustration and consist of several sheets of paper cut away in such a manner as to give light and shade to the design by altering pressure on the block. There are also mechanical overlays, made by an etching process.

Over-run: To turn over words from one line to the next for several successive lines after an insertion or a deletion.

Outer forme: The pages of type which fall on the outside of a sheet.

Page: One side of a leaf. Abbreviated to p. with pp. in the plural.

Pagination: The numbering of a book with a number on each page.

Paste-up: A dummy made for the printer's guidance in which galley proofs and/or block proofs are pasted.

Perfecting machine: A machine which has two impression cylinders and prints both sides of a sheet at one operation.

Pica: A measurement approximately ⅙ of an inch. While formerly 'pica' referred to a variable size of type, it is often, though incorrectly, used to denote the 12-pt. em.

Pie: Type which has been accidentally mixed.

Photogravure: A mechanical intaglio process superseding the hand-engraved copperplate.

Plate: An electro or stereo. Also the name given to an insetted illustration in a book.

Point System: The point is the standard of typographical measurement in use today in England and America, and 72 points measure 0·9962″, approximately 1″. Every body size, therefore, is an exact multiple or sub-multiple of every other body size.

Preliminary pages: Those pages of a book containing the matter preceding the main body of the text, such as the half-title, contents page, introduction, etc.

Press proofs: The final proofs of any work before printing.

Proof: A trial print from type or plates.

Proof-reading: This consists of checking the set-up matter from the author's manuscript, and marking the necessary corrections to make the proof correct and tally with the MS. The proof is also marked to conform with the house style of the printer.

Pull: Another name for a proof.

Quadrats: Spaces. Pieces of blank metal less than type height used to fill up spaces and short lines in a page of type. Six sizes are supplied with every fount of type, and in width they are all fractions of the em. They comprise: (i) em quadrat, the body, (ii) en quadrat, ½ body, (iii) thick space, ⅓ body, (iv) middle space, ¼ body, (v) thin space, ⅕ body, and (vi) hair space, 1/12 body approximately.

Quarter bound: A style of binding in which the back is of different material from the sides.

Quarto: A size obtained when a sheet is folded into four. Abbreviated to 4to.

Quire: Twenty-four sheets of paper.

Ream: A term denoting a number of sheets of paper ranging from 480 to 516.

Recto: Any right-hand page of a book, that is, odd-numbered.

Register: The exact adjustment of pages back-to-back in printing the second side of a sheet, so that in folding, the margins will all be correct. In printing work with two or more colours, the positioning of one colour in its correct relation with the rest is known as 'register'.

Retree: A term used to denote slightly defective sheets of paper.

Rivers: Unsightly streaks of white space which appear in pages of printing, caused by over-spacing and by spaces appearing immediately above and below one another.

Royal: A standard size of printing paper measuring 20″ × 25″.

Rules: Type-high strips of metal of various widths cut to standard lengths. These are used to print straight lines. Some thicker rules have engraved surfaces which print in a design, and some are cut to show a wavy line surface. Many varieties are obtainable in brass, type-metal and zinc.

Run: The number of copies required from each forme.

Running head-line: The heading to a page.

Run on: A sentence continued in the same line as the previous one, not a distinct paragraph. Chapters which do not start on a fresh page are said to 'run on'. Run on also refers to additional copies printed at the same time as the original printing. These are naturally charged at a much lower price.

Sans serif: A class of types which is characterized by the absence of serifs and the construction of the letters from strokes of equal thickness.

Script: A term applied to any face cut to resemble handwriting.

Serifs: The finishing strokes at the top and bottom of a letter.

Set: This is the amount of lateral spacing between letters and depends on the thickness of body apportioned to each character. Thus types are spoken of as having 'wide' set or 'narrow' set.

Setting type: This is a recognized term for composing type.

Set-off: The impression made on successive sheets of paper by the wet ink taken from one another, which can be avoided by interleaving the printed sheets with blank sheets of paper, or more generally by spraying.

Shank: Sometimes called the stem. It is the exactly rectangular main body of the type.

Signature: In bookwork, the first page of each section bears a distinguishing letter or figure called a 'signature' which proceeds in order throughout the sections of a book, and thus acts as a guide in gathering. Hence the term is often used by the binder to mean the section itself.

Small capitals: Book founts contain a series of 'small capitals' in most sizes which are smaller than full capitals. SMALL CAPITALS, FULL CAPITALS. They are indicated by double underlinings.

Sorts: Each individual type character is known to the printer as a 'sort'.

Special sorts: These are types which are not usually included in a fount and are supplied on request, such as fractions, musical signs, superior and inferior letters and figures, etc.

Spine: The back of the binding case of the book which is visible when it is on the shelf.

Standing type: Type which has been printed and is kept in store in readiness for reprinting.

Stereotype: A replica from type or a block, cast in metal from a papier-mâché mould.

Superior letters or figures: Small letters and figures cast on the shoulder of the type so that they print above the level of such letters as s or p, thus: s^a, p^1. *Inferior* letters and figures are also obtainable, and these print below the main part of the letter, thus: a_a, b_1.

Swash letters: Old face italic types with decorative flourishes.

Swelled rules: A class of ornamental rule thick in the centre and graduating down to fine lines at each end.

Tail: Binder's term for the bottom margin of a page.

Tellers: Small right angled marks printed to show the binder the positions for tipping the plates on mounts.

GLOSSARY

Tint blocks: Blocks or surfaces used for printing flat background colours.

Tipping in: An illustration or other loose plate, cut to the size of the book, is said to be tipped in when it is pasted at its back margin to the page following.

Titling: Founts of capitals cast so as to occupy the whole of the body size of the type, leaving no beard at the foot.

Type area: The specified amount of space on a page to be filled with type.

Type height: All types are cast to a standard height which is 0·918″ in England. Blocks are mounted to the same height, so that the 'height-to-paper' is uniform in a forme which contains both type and illustration blocks.

Upper case: The top one of a pair of type cases which contains the capital and small capital letters. Also the part of the fount containing the capitals and small capitals.

Verso: The reverse or back of a leaf. All the left-hand, even-numbered pages of a book.

Vignette: A small illustration or decoration which is not squared up or enclosed by a border.

Warping: Bindings may warp for a variety of reasons. Sometimes the endpapers have been attached the wrong way of the grain: sometimes the moisture content of the boards is too high.

Watermark: A design impressed into sheets of paper during manufacture which serves to identify the products of the various paper mills.

Whole bound: A volume bound entirely in one material.

Work and turn: A method of imposing work in which the matter is printed in its entirety on both sides of the sheet in such a way as to yield two complete copies after cutting.

Wove: A term applied to papers made on an ordinary web in which the wires are woven, used in contradistinction to *laid.*

Wrong fount: An error in composing caused by sorts of one fount becoming mixed with another and appearing in the matter set.

SELECT HAND-LIST

Unless otherwise stated the books listed have been published in London.

BOOKS

The Printed Book, by H. G. Aldis. Cambridge University Press. 1942.

An Encyclopaedia of Type Faces, by W. T. Berry and A. F. Johnson. Blandford Press. 1953.

An Approach to Type, by John R. Biggs. Blandford Press. 1949.

The Use of Type: the Practice of Typography, by John R. Biggs. Blandford Press. 1954.

The Illustration of Books, by David Bland (Second Edition). Faber & Faber. 1962.

Paper and its Relationship to Books, by R. H. Clapperton. Dent. 1934.

Authors' and Printers' Dictionary, by F. Howard Collins (10th Edition). Oxford University Press. 1960.

An Essay on Typography, by Eric Gill (Second Edition). Sheed and Ward. 1936.

XIXth Century Ornamented Types and Title Pages, by Nicolete Gray. Faber & Faber. 1938.

The Printing of Books, by Holbrook Jackson. Cassell. 1938.

The Making of Books, by Séan Jennett. Faber & Faber. 1951.

Decorative Initial Letters, by A. F. Johnson. Cresset Press. 1931.

Type Designs, by A. F. Johnson. Grafton. 1934.

The Printer, His Customers and His Men, by John Johnson. Dent. 1933.

Drawing for Illustration, by Lynton Lamb. Oxford University Press. 1962.

Modern Book Design, by Ruari McLean. Faber & Faber. 1958.

A Publisher on Book Production, by Richard de la Mare. Dent. 1936.

The Printing of Poetry. A paper read before the Double Crown Club by Walter de la Mare. London. 1931.

G. B. Bodoni's Preface to the Manuale Tipografico *of 1818*, translated into English with an Introduction by H. V. Marrot. Elkin Mathews. 1925.

Leaves Out of Books. (An Album of leaves cut from eighty typical current Books.) Monotype Corporation. 1938.

A Brief Survey of Printing History and Practice, by Stanley Morison and Holbrook Jackson. The Fleuron. 1923.

Four Centuries of Fine Printing, by Stanley Morison. Benn. 1924.

Modern Fine Printing, by Stanley Morison. Benn. 1925.

John Bell 1745–1831, by Stanley Morison. Cambridge University Press. 1930.

First Principles of Typography, by Stanley Morison. Cambridge University Press. 1936.

The Art of Printing, by Stanley Morison. British Academy. 1937.

English Prayer, Books by Stanley Morison. Cambridge University Press. 1943.

The Typographic Arts, by Stanley Morison. Sylvan Press. 1949.

The Art of the Book, by Bernard Newdigate. The Studio. 1938.

Rules for Compositors and Readers at the Oxford University Press (36th Edition). Humphrey Milford. 1957.

A History of the Old English Letter Foundries, by T. B. Reed, edited by A. F. Johnson. Faber & Faber. 1952.

Modern and Historical Typography, by Imre Reiner. St. Gall: Zollikofer. 1946.

The Growth of the Book Jacket, by C. Rosner. Sylvan Press. 1954.

Printing Explained, by H. Simon and H. Carter. Dryad. 1931.

Printing of Today. Edited by Oliver Simon and Julius Rodenberg. Peter Davies. 1928.

Five Hundred Years of Printing, by S. H. Steinberg (Second Edition). Faber & Faber. 1959.

How to Plan Print, by J. C. Tarr (Second Edition). Crosby Lockwood. 1949.

Type for Print, by David Thomas. Whitaker. 1947.

Designing Books, by Jan Tschichold. New York: Wittenborn Schultz Inc. 1951.

In the Day's Work, by Daniel Berkeley Updike. Humphrey Milford. 1924.

Printing Types, Their History, Forms and Use, by Daniel Berkeley Updike (Second Edition). Humphrey Milford. 1937.

The Practice of Typography: *A Treatise on Title-pages*, by Theodore Low De Vinne, New York; The Century Co. 1914.

The Practice of Typography: *Correct Composition*, by Theodore Low De Vinne, New York; The Century Co. 1916.

Methods of Book Design, by Hugh Williamson. Oxford University Press. 1956.

PERIODICALS

The Fleuron, A Journal of Typography
>Nos. I–IV edited by Oliver Simon. The Fleuron. 1923–5.
>
>Nos. V–VI edited by Stanley Morison. Cambridge University Press. 1926–30.

Signature, A Quadrimestrial of Typography and Graphic Arts. Edited by Oliver Simon. Signature. 1935–40.

Signature, New Series, 1946.

The Monotype Recorder
>Nos. 212–13 (Double Number) 1926. 'Pierre Simon Fournier and XVIIIth Century French Typography', by Paul Beaujon.
>
>No. 228. 1929. 'Tendencies in British Book Printing.'
>
>Vol. 26. No. 221. 1927. 'The Baskerville Types.'
>
>Vol. 30. No. 240. 1931. 'Towards a Nomenclature for Letter Forms', by Joseph Thorp.
>
>Vol. 32. No. 1. 1933. 'On the Choice of Type Faces', by Paul Beaujon.
>
>Vol. 32. No. 3. 1933. 'A Printer Considers the Book', by Francis Meynell.
>
>Vol. 34. No. 2. 1935. 'The Neglected School Book', by R. D. Morss.
>
>Vol. 35. No. 2. 1936 (Annual Book Number). 'The Book of Verse', by Paul Beaujon.
>
>Vol. 36. No. 1. 1937. 'Black Letter: Its History and Use.'

Typography. Shenval Press. 1936–39.

Alphabet and Image. Shenval Press. 1948–52.

Motif. Shenval Press. 1958–

Typographica. Lund Humphries. 1949–

Book Design and Production. Thames Publishing Co. 1958–

The Penrose Annual, published by Lund Humphries and edited by Allan Delafons, is a yearly review of technical developments with articles on book design and production.

SUBJECT INDEX

SUBJECT INDEX

163